An Idiot and a Broad

Stephanie Hansell

An Idiot
and a
Broad

MEMOIRS

Cirencester

Published by Memoirs

MEMOIRS
PUBLISHING

Memoirs Books

25 Market Place, Cirencester, Gloucestershire, GL7 2NX
info@memoirsbooks.co.uk www.memoirspublishing.com

ISBN 978-1-909020-19-1

Printed in England

Contents

Introduction

INTRODUCTION

This book is about our world trip. I wrote it because I wanted to share our experiences with others. It has been written in a tongue-in-cheek way and is not to be taken too seriously – I hope it will make you laugh along the way.

I could not have done this trip without the company and the love of my lovely husband Tony (who also put up all the money). We enjoyed every minute of it and we hope you enjoy reading about it. Hopefully it may inspire you to go travelling.

Thank you to Andy and Sarah & family, Doreen, and Margaret and Joe. Thank you to my wonderful family and friends for always being there for me. Thanks Wes and Nicky, you were my inspiration to write this. And a special thank you to my mam, who we love very much.

Chapter One

AN EXPENSIVE TRIP TO TOWN

Tony and I had always talked about travelling the world one day, and now the opportunity seemed right. So we started planning. Only in our heads at first, but once we started to talk about all the things we wanted to do and the places we wanted to see, our enthusiasm took over.

After seventeen years of married life we were getting used to each other and knew we had a lot in common. Tony's 32 years in the fire service had given him many skills, not just playing cards and snooker. So after talking things through, we began looking up some of the places on the internet.

One of the things we both wanted to get involved in was voluntary work with rescued animals. Then a trip to the jungle began to look interesting, though some of the destinations were quite expensive, and volunteers were expected to work for at least a month. We checked out several places of sanctuary for big cats. I'm talking lions, tigers, leopards and others, the ones that would rip your head off and eat you for breakfast.

I must confess that the idea of living in the jungle scared me. Nor did either of us have any experience of working with animals. The closest I had got was when I had fed a camel at Edinburgh Zoo at the age of about eight. It slavered on my hand, and it had the worst halitosis you could imagine. I never wanted to feed one again after that.

We went into Newcastle one day in April 2010 to visit Primark and dropped into Trailfinders while we were there. Two hours later we came out looking at each other with terrified expressions. We had really dropped ourselves in at the deep end. We had set up a seven-month tour of the far side of the world, taking in Hong Kong, Thailand, Vietnam, Cambodia, Malaysia, Singapore, Australia, New Zealand and South America. Not exactly a weekend in Blackpool. We had booked to leave on October 31st.

Our little shopping trip had become rather expensive. We would have to rent the house out, sell the car, get the necessary injections, redirect the post, pack our stuff into storage, and let everyone know. Nothing too major!

It was quite a lot to take in, so we went straight to the pub for a few pints to talk it over. We soon realised after bumping into too many people we knew that we weren't going to discuss anything. All we were going to do was get pissed.

Four hours later we remembered we had left the car parked in town. A great start. We had to get up early the next morning and catch the Metro into town to collect it. I had parked in my sister's private bay, so at least I wasn't facing a three hundred and fifty quid ticket. Neither had I been wheel-clamped by those kind people from Newcastle City Council.

One of the first things on the list was to make an appointment for our jabs. It quickly came round and we found ourselves sitting in the waiting room of our local GP surgery being patronised by the nurse, who told us in no uncertain terms that we would have to give her a detailed itinerary of our trip before she could even start to consider giving us the necessary injections. I think it would have been easier to get a prescription for heroin. We were sent packing.

We returned a week later, better prepared. After studying the map and the areas where we would be going the nurse decided we needed diphtheria, tetanus, polio, typhoid, hepatitis A, malaria and Japanese encephalitis. The malaria dose, at least, was in the form of tablets. We were literally ready to take on the world, though I never did understand why the Japanese encephalitis jab was necessary. I had no intention of fighting the Japanese or anyone else for that matter. I just wanted a peaceful trip.

Now we had to sort out visas to visit all those countries. After much running around and many phone calls, we got everything sorted in a matter of a few months and were ready for the off. We got the house spick and span and spent hours doing the gardens ready for our tenants. The search for tenants wasn't long - the estate agents found a nice couple who didn't have any kids, enjoyed going to church and loved gardening. We couldn't get them to sign quick enough. They sounded too good to be true, and I was wondering if my house was going to be turned into a cannabis farm.

We bought repellent spray and acquired a mosquito net from my sister Sharron, who had bought it for a trip to India but had never used it because there was no hook on the ceiling. Personally I would suggest that the management get a few hooks rigged up straight away on account of the mosquitoes being the size of small wasps.

The time was fast approaching, and we had moved in with my mother as the new tenants had now moved into our house. I had left home to work in Edinburgh when I was seventeen and hadn't really been back since, so I wasn't sure if this was going to be the biggest challenge, or travelling around the world. We had to be up at 5 am for the airport, and neither of us really slept much. My mam got up and had a cup of tea with us while we waited for my sister and brother-in-law. They picked my other sister up on the way.

I had already spoken to my brother, sister-in-law and the kids, AKA Ronnie and Reggie, on the phone. My sister was on time picking us up, which was a miracle in itself – the first of many wonders of the world I was about to witness!

It was soon time to go, and we kissed my mam at home because she couldn't face coming to the airport and saying goodbye (plus she wanted to get straight back to bed).

There was very little traffic on the road at that time in the morning, so we seemed to get there in record time, although considering that Sharron could give Jenson Button driving lessons we probably did. It was like being in an episode of Back to the Future. We were in, seat belts on, and then whoosh, we were there. The late Jimmy Savile would have struggled to clunk-click that fast.

Loads of cuddling and tears, then we were on our way. We had been putting our plans together for so long now that it seemed strange that we were finally about to put them to the test.

I remember going to Scarborough once as a kid and being put off by how long the journey was. Thankfully I realised as I got older that it was actually only a few hours, so I was well prepared for the long flights. First things first, we got checked in. My rucksack weighed 11 kilos and Tony's 13. We might have packed too much stuff!

We headed straight into the duty-free shop to get as many free samples as possible. A last few pints now in Newcastle, just in case the beer was crap. The Toon V Mackam match was on - we couldn't believe it (a Newcastle United v. Sunderland derby.)

I had told Tony to leave his watch at home because the strap was too tight and kept springing off his wrist, but he takes no notice of me and I noticed he still had it on.

The flight from Newcastle was under an hour and we had a connecting flight from Heathrow. We managed not to have a domestic in Heathrow, so we were doing well. Seven months to go. Bring it on!

We boarded our flight in a mixture of excitement and trepidation at what lay ahead. Here is the diary of our trip, complete with all the tantrums, fights and other escapades we got up to on the way. Some of the things we experienced and witnessed were so incredible that I don't think we will ever think the same way again. In short - we had the time of our lives.

Chapter Two

HONG KONG

31ST OCTOBER 2010

The flight from Heathrow to Hong Kong took 10 hours and 50 minutes. It seemed to go on forever (my sister could have driven us there faster) but the free drink is always an added bonus. As the stewards pass continuously throughout the journey giving out meals and ice creams, then more snacks and drinks, we wondered if we would be able to get out of the seat when we landed.

After we'd been in the air for a while darkness started to fall and the lights were dimmed in the cabin. I hate this part of the flight, as I can never get comfortable. The stewardess asked 'Is everything all right?' to which I replied 'I can't get comfortable'. She leaned over and pushed a button, which made my seat go back. 'Is that better?' she said, smiling. I smiled back and said 'Yes, I'm sure I will sleep great now, it's reclined at least four inches. You'll probably have to wake me up when we get there.' I think she thought I was serious!

The flight reminded me of the times we used to go to Whitby as kids for our holidays, because as a child the journey took just as long, or it seemed like it did. Off we would go with my Aunty Mona and Uncle Billy's tent all packed in the back of Uncle Billy's green Transit van, which was fitted out with bench seats and curtains (they were the posh in laws). We bumped up and down, shunted from the top of the seat to the bottom, all the way to Whitby, where everybody spoke funny and where Dracula lived.

6

No seat belts then. We negotiated hairpin bends, heart-stopping dips and sheer cliff drops as my dad drove us off to this foreign land. 'Are we there yet, Dad?' was the chorus every ten minutes. 'No, shut up!'

My mam used to remind us that it was a long way and our dad needed to concentrate on the road. I knew my dad was a good driver, because when he used to come in from the club on a Saturday night he would get Rosemary and Sharron and me in the van and ask us to keep an eye out for the police. He used to say 'If you see the coppers make sure you tell me, 'cos they want me to drive for them and I'm happy at Park Cakes.'

I can remember my dad working for that cake company and I loved our Sunday tea. No way were the coppers taking my dad to drive for them, so I was extra vigilant. It used to make me feel so important, like a ten-year-old private eye. I believed his story for years. We always managed to get back with our Chinese cuisine of curry, rice and chips. I was cultured from a very young age!

After a mammoth journey we finally arrived in Whitby. We used to get excited at seeing the Abbey on the cliff top and we couldn't wait to get there. But it still looked miles away. I remember our Sharron and Rosemary trying their best to scare me when we spotted the Abbey, putting their arms up and showing their teeth from under their top lip. I was scared all right, but now in hindsight they were just doing a shit impersonation of a vampire. They looked like female versions of Mr Ed, the TV talking horse. My dad used to shout at them 'If the wind changes, your face will stay like that'. I used to see old people with no teeth and faces like they were gurning, and think they had never listened to their dads.

We camped at a place called Stoupcross Farm year after year, and we loved it. When we arrived at the camp site we couldn't wait to get out and play. We only had a blow-up dolphin and a pair of baseball boots that Sharron and I had to share, but those were the days. I had them on on day one, and I remember walking in an exaggerated way so that people would notice them. I would pretend that I had hurt my leg just so people would say 'Oh I like your boots', but they never did. They probably thought I had a calliper on my leg under my trousers.

My dad wanted to get the tent up before the day was gone. Little did I realise that it was only two and a half hours since we had left home, and we had left at ten o'clock. We ate our meals outside in the open air, choked by the overwhelming smell of cow shit, though to us it just added to the feeling of being 'abroad'.

One year my dad pitched the tent on a manure heap by accident and we spent the night holding our breath. Our eyes stung from the acrid smell of cow piss until we could move the next morning. We should have known something was up when we saw a big space and no one on it.

The next day, after several hours of working out the poles again, we managed to shift spots. I seem to remember that there were more poles than on a scaffolding job on Durham Cathedral or working on the London Olympics. They were all cleverly marked with coloured electrical tape so that it would be easy to put it up, but of course this idea never worked. My dad could never remember if the yellow went with the blue or the red with the black, so several hours later we were housed in a tent with such an odd shape that Walt Disney couldn't have drawn it.

Off my dad would go for bread and other supplies, and he would always come back smelling of John Smith's. I would then lie in bed at night thinking that the roof looked a bit dodgy and suspecting that the yellow might possible have gone with the red after all, but I never mentioned this for fear that my mother would rip the whole lot down while biting into her hand (she did this when she was annoyed, a bit like an adult teething ring I suppose) and say we were all going home.

If it rained you must never, ever, touch the canvas, or it would leak. I remember Sharron chasing me into the tent and I accidentally touched the roof. I then had to sit with a bucket to catch the drips for two hours. I remember thinking it would cost hundreds to repair, because once the canvas was touched that was it. People used to tell stories about having to have their tent rewaxed after the seal was broken because it had been touched when wet. We used to walk around inside avoiding the canvas, like that game where you guide the hoop through the copper wire - of course you always touched it and made it buzz. Those were the days.

I have actually been back to that place with a group of friends since, and the drive has no hairpin bends, heart-stopping cliffs or sheer drops – it's just a straight road. What imaginations we have as kids. Also we have a modern tent now, with only two poles.

My big sister Rosemary was too old to be playing with us and too young to be doing adult stuff, so we used to drop her off at the laundrette while we all went off to the pictures, usually to see Chitty Chitty Bang Bang for the eighth time. Once she decided to sleep in the van on the floor between the seats. The next morning when she opened the curtains she found she was parked in Whitby and my dad was in the 'John Smith's' shop getting the bread.

The weather always seemed great - you never remember rain as a kid. We ate out sometimes, at least if eating fish and chips on the beach counts as eating out. I remember once going into a restaurant and sitting down, and being dead excited when we looked at our reflections in the silver spoons. Five minutes later we heard my dad telling the young waiter that he could shove the fish and chips up his arse, his restaurant was highway robbery and at least Dick Turpin wore a mask. I remember years later watching Top of the Pops and seeing Adam Ant and asking my dad if he was Dick Turpin. My dad would always answer by saying 'Wa breedin' a nation of friggin' idiots', so I was still none the wiser about whether Adam Ant and Dick Turpin were the same person.

My dad always used to say what he thought. He once said to Jackie, my brother's wife, 'What's wrong wi ya face love?' 'Nothing' was Jackie's reply. 'Well it's all swollen' he said. We still laugh about it now because Jackie was just a podgy-faced lass, but it would have been enough to make her turn and run a mile - which I'm glad to say she didn't.

The next café we stopped at was advertising a 'Pensioners' Special' which my dad complained about, saying 'those bloody pensioners get everything'. In my young mind I thought it meant they would be getting help eating their dinners, because when you're only a kid anyone over the age of twenty looks about seventy. So while my dad was thinking of where else we could eat, we watched the pensioners sitting inside eating their 'Pensioner's Special', which was just fish and chips. They were tucking in with such gusto that there were practically sparks coming off the cutlery. My mam used to say that the pensioners didn't eat much, but their plates were piled high and they never left any. We were like window lickers and bloody starving. In fact I would have let Sharron wear the boots for a bag of chips.

Anyway, back to the flight. It seemed to go on forever. I sat next to an Aussie called Dave, who turned out to be sociable and friendly. I was so glad, nothing worse than sitting next to a bore or someone who is deodorant challenged.

We didn't seem to be on the flight for long when our in-flight meal arrived. It was the usual airline food, it fills you but you always wonder how. There is no way I could cook a meal that would fit into a little aluminium box. You take the lid off and say 'Oh, that looks nice'. It might be because you can only eat it with your elbows tucked in and your arms flapping from side to side like a penguin. You keep the cheese till last, sometimes even for a few hours just in case the next in-flight snack is not to your taste.

The couple sitting over from us were not keeping theirs but trying their best to open it; it was vacuum-packed, which makes the task even harder. I got the giggles watching them. They kept trying to find the little bit on the end that you peel back. Big sighs and then they would try again. The glasses were on, the glasses were off, he snatched it off her, she snatched it back. I thought at one point she was going to eat it with the plastic still on, but she didn't.

Fifteen minutes later and they were still trying to open it, having both put their glasses on to check which end you open they had resorted to a two-man job, him holding it and her frantically trying to cut it open with a plastic knife. If she'd gone any faster she would be in possession of a lethal weapon, as the plastic on the knife was getting sharper. I wasn't convinced she wouldn't use on her husband if he dared to snatch the cheese out of her hand again.

1ST NOVEMBER

When we landed in Hong Kong Tony switched his phone on to receive one message: Toon 5 - Scum 1. (It's the hatred that makes our derby game the best in the world). Obviously the text had to be from our mate John Mac.

Almost immediately we spotted a little Chinese fella in a Toon top - good start. We had a pick-up from the airport, so we enjoyed the journey into the western district of the city. I have never seen so many high-rise blocks or so many people all in one place. The river was stuffed with ships, each carrying hundreds of containers piled eight high. They looked like match boxes, and it was impossible to appreciate the actual size of the ship.

The smog was thick across the water and visibility was limited. On the drive through Hong Kong we caught sight of many shops selling strange items and open-air butchers with unidentified meat hanging up. I knew then I was going to lose weight. It was right in the heart of town on the main shopping street, a weird place. There were some very expensive shops next to the hotel, along with a couple of buildings that looked like slums on the other side.

We wanted to treat ourselves for the first bit of the journey, so we booked an expensive hotel where the staff were lovely, though very formal. My first impressions of Hong Kong were ambiguous. I saw more things I didn't like than I did on the short journey. Hopefully I was going to become a bit more cultured along the way.

I was knackered by the jet lag, but I knew it was best to keep going. Our hotel had a rooftop pool, which was nice, but the buildings around it shaded most of the pool, so the water was very cold. Still it was nice to relax and read, and the views were magnificent, if slightly blighted by the pollution.

After a while we decided to go for a walk, and headed into town for a look around. The walk took only about half an hour and there was plenty to see en route. We saw some weird stuff - reptiles on sticks fried and ready to eat, no doubt with a few hundreds-and-thousands to 'bring out the flavour'. The only thing I would be doing with that would be bringing it back up.

Good beer though, and cheap. We stumbled into a back lane in search of some food, finding that nothing at all on the menu resembling anything we had ever seen in our lives. It was a case of match the picture with the food, but first you had to guess what the picture was of - it was like a pissed Pictionary quiz.

We went into what looked like a noodle café and struggled with the menu. We didn't have a clue what we were about to get, but it arrived anyway looking like something even the dog would turn down. The taste actually wasn't too bad, and it wasn't until we had dipped our fingers into the little bowl that we realised it was soup. I blamed the jet lag.

When the plate of what was supposed to be noodles arrived at our table Tony got stuck in. There was an elderly man sitting behind us who was slurping so loudly it sounded like Dyno Rod had a serious job on. It is of course customary for the Chinese to show appreciation for their food, and he made the point by swiftly following up with the loudest belch, like the sort you do when you have just gulped a can of Coke. I would have been sent off the table at home for doing that. We weren't even allowed to talk at table and my dad used to bang his knife on the side of your plate to shut you up. I used to look at the pieces of potato flying through the air in slow motion as I moved my plate around in the hope they wouldn't land on it, which they always did. I would look at my dad's dinner, which he used to mash all together into a brown runny mess on his plate, and think he just doesn't get the idea of presentation. A la carte would have been pointless in our house.

My brother James and I once got the giggles, which resulted in my dad shaking like an epileptic and my mother throwing her dinner up the wall. My dad refused to lose face and stayed at the table while my mother stormed out. As the Yorkshire pudding slid down the wall, James and I thought of people dying and tried to think of sad things to help us to stop laughing, but it never worked and we were soon hysterical. When you have the giggles even sad things make you hysterical.

My dad eventually stormed out, saying his favourite phrase again, 'Wa breedin' a bunch of friggin' idiots!' We still laugh about it to this day when we reminisce about my dad, who has since sadly passed away.

From our hotel window there was a block of flats directly facing us, 15 storeys high. Each one had a washing line attached to a small wooden rack hanging out of the window. It looked like a scene from Beirut. I wondered how many people actually lived in them - my guess would be hundreds. The washing lines were all full, and I watched a lady putting out her laundry as she leaned out of the top window with a peg in one hand and a pair of jeans in the other. My heart was in my mouth just watching. I wonder how many times people are hit by an old stray pair of pants or jeans that fall off. What a nightmare having to run down 15 flights of stairs hoping your clothes are still there when you reach the bottom. I know a few areas back home where someone would have them on quicker than you could make it down the first stair.

I was taking the photographs, as Tony hasn't grasped the idea of getting head, feet and arms in. Point and shoot is his idea. I say to him 'You have to get the whole picture in.'

'Why, I know what the rest looks like.'

'How?'

'Cos it's in my head.'

'Yes, but when you show someone the picture they can't see what's in your head.'

'Well, I won't show anyone.'

'Over the years you'll forget.'

'I won't.'

'So why bother taking photos then?'

'So I can look at them and remember.'

'I thought you would never forget.'

'Well I might.'

'Exactly, that's why you're not taking any more photos.'

2ND NOVEMBER

The smog was pretty bad here today, a bit like Middlesbrough but with higher buildings and less unemployment (tongue in cheek, I like Middlesbrough)

Pretty much the same as yesterday, had breakfast in the hotel restaurant and then chilled for a little while at the pool. At the pool were the two thinnest women in Hong Kong. I wanted to feed them up. They looked like they were living on 200 calories a day each.

We walked along to Hollywood Street, which is the place to go for bars and fortunately not too far from our hotel. There was weird stuff in the shops en route to the bars, tiger claws and skins, reptiles on sticks and deer's foetuses - they believe the deer foetus to be of medicinal value. It's incredible that the Chinese are so advanced in their inventions and architecture, yet can still be so cruel to animals. There are many open-air butcher's shops, each with a menacing-looking Chinese man sitting on a plastic chair outside. We try and guess what the meat products are and are none the wiser. Some of the meat is too small to be lamb so we think it could possibly be dog or cat. Mind you I know a few people who would gladly string little Kitty up when they discover their pansies have been dug up and replaced by buried shit. Anyway I'm not even sure if either is a delicacy here in Hong Kong. Either way he looks menacing enough with the machetes hanging behind him. He doesn't look like he would be intimidated by anyone.

3RD NOVEMBER

There were a few big girls at the pool today, which was a welcoming sight. I hated the idea of the breakfast buffet going to waste. Still didn't go in the water though, it was far too cold.

Went to the river and watched the cargo ships loading and unloading the huge containers. They looked like toys next to the backdrop of the massive buildings.

Tomorrow we are travelling to Bangkok to begin the start of our real backpacking experience. We have escaped the 'red shirt' riots, so it's pretty safe now.

Chapter Three

BANGKOK AND THAILAND

4TH NOVEMBER – 8TH NOVEMBER

Back in the airport again, the first of many to come. We were early for our flight but got checked in quick and got through to the departure lounge, where there were loads of old men with Thai girls flying back to Bangkok. No doubt the men will be a few quid lighter for their experience.

We landed in Bangkok and stayed in the real backpacker area right in the centre of the hustle and bustle, facing Khosan Road, called the Rambrutti. It is constantly packed with people coming and going at all times of day and night. Surprisingly there are quite a few older travellers, as well as everything you could possibly want to buy here. The streets are full of silvery stainless-steel carts selling everything from noodles and pancakes to locusts and crickets with scorpion, all fried and ready to eat. We opted for the scorpion and handed over our few bhat, to find it tasted like shit. I wouldn't recommend eating them before a hot date unless you have no intention of smiling. I needed to get my hair cut but I was thinking that I might just shave it all off, because I'm away for so long.

Having visited Thailand before we were determined not to have anything to do with the 'tuk-tuk' (rickshaw) drivers, but five minutes later I was talking to the driver of a lovely blue one - don't ask why, stupidity is the only explanation. I asked him to take us to the railway station (we had to book our overnight train to Chang Mai anyway so thought we might as well go by 'tuk-tuk' as a taxi).

Five minutes later we were being taken to his 'friend's' jewellery shop, then on to his 'friend's' tailor's shop. After inhaling more fumes than a butane gas addict Tony got annoyed and told him to take us to the railway station. The driver said he would, great we thought but then we stopped and he told us to get out for our train tickets. We looked and saw that we were outside a tourist information shop.

'This is not the station?'

'Yes, you take ticket from here.'

We went inside, only to find it was another 'friend's' shop! After a conversation in Thai we were told we could not get a ticket because the train was fully booked, but we could fly for £100 each. The disadvantage of not being tanned yet seems to give the tuk-tuk drivers the authority to try and rip you off and basically take the piss. We told the girl behind the desk that we were not interested in flying and walked out. She very nearly got a quick back hander as she attempted to grab my arm on the way out, but fortunately for her she let go.

We got back in the tuk-tuk and Tony said to the driver through gritted teeth 'Take us to the 'f-u-c-k-i-n-g r-a-i-l-w-a-y s-t-a-t-i-o-n'! Imagine getting in a taxi at home and them taking you everywhere but where you want to go. The casualty department would be busy.

Anyway we continued on our journey from hell, dodging in and out of traffic with our fingers crossed and hearts in our mouths. I smiled at Tony and he said 'I can't believe I listened to you and got in this fucking tuk-tuk!'

When the driver mentioned visiting a temple, Tony gave him the 'I'm gonna rip your fucking head off' look and he promptly drove around the corner and blatantly switched off his engine. He jumped from the tuk-tuk holding his head in his hands and said 'Oh I Blake down'. We looked at each other and laughed, and it wasn't a funny laugh but the laugh of anger. Tony said to him 'Well you can fuck right off if you think you're getting any money, you little twat'. We got out and walked away, half expecting to be followed by an angry gang of Thai relatives - as everyone we seemed to meet appeared to be his cousin - but he just drove off without his fare.

We walked along the street and hailed the local bus down just to get away. Four stops later we were at the station. Of course we should have done that in the first place - first lesson learned. Outside the railway station there are many official-looking people who will try and sell you a ticket for your journey, but we knew not to use them but to go straight to the desk and buy our tickets there. Of course they were not sold out. The Thais are experts at ripping you off.

When we looked at our tickets we found that we were going to be facing each other on the top bunks. We were a bit worried when the lady behind the counter stood up and looked at us both, giggled and said something to her colleague, then said 'velly small beds'.

We jumped on to a local bus that said 'Kohsan Road' on the front and within about ten minutes we were back at the top of our street and saw the same driver touting for business as, surprise surprise, his tuk-tuk was repaired. He smiled as if to say 'I tried' and we smiled back to say 'nice one, you got us fair and square'. Twat!

We were staying not far from the Grand Palace, and the art and architecture are beautiful. It's on the Chao Phraya River and the palace covers more than 1.5 sq km. The dress code is very strict - men have to wear trousers and no vests and women are to wear nothing skimpy or too revealing and have their shoulders covered, so my mini, boob tube and high heels were out the question.

It was the Newcastle v Arsenal match that night, so we watched it in the street, where plastic tables and chairs had been put out and electrical cables had been rigged up to a large TV screen. The beer was dead cheap, Chang lager, strong and blows you head off. I had decided earlier that afternoon that I would shave my hair off after all and got the shears. It felt very liberating to be able to do it. I have had it very short once before and had it dyed; it was supposed to be blonde but turned out ginger, so instead of looking cool and edgy I just looked like Butch Dingle from Emmerdale. Thankfully like last time it will grow back. This time it looked better.

I had been talked into getting a henna tattoo on my arm by a lady sitting on the street. Tony asked why I didn't bargain over the price. I told him that when you get something on your arm that's going to be on for two weeks you want it to be what you have asked for. If I had bartered too much I might have ended up with a penis and balls like the ones you see painted on walls by graffiti artists.

Tony laughed. 'She could have modelled it on mine, what do you think she would say to that if I showed her?'

'Oh, that looks like a penis only smaller.'

'Very funny.'

'I wasn't trying to be.'

Newcastle 1, Arsenal 0 - great result, especially when you have watched it with a load of Thais who support Arsenal along with a few Cockneys. Even better when Tony stood up and shouted 'TOON, TOON TOON ARMY!' It's a bit out of character. Personally I'm blaming the Chang Lager.

When I ordered my 'flied lice' I said to the lady 'no meat please'. She looked at her friend and said something in Thai which I couldn't understand but loosely translated I think meant 'No meat? Is this idiot joking, does she really think we use more than one pan?'

That night we visited a pub to watch the infamous 'ping pong show', purely, as Tony says, in the name of culture. The ping pong show is basically women shooting ping pong balls out of their vaginas with great speed and accuracy, aiming at targets that were set up on the stage. A birthday cake with candles and a couple of goldfish bowls were among the things she had to aim for.

Contestant number one took to the stage in her 'uniform', which was a bikini top. I suppose the ball would have gotten caught in the gusset of her knickers if she had left them on. Anyway we were impressed, as every ping pong ball hit the candle on the cake and she got a few in the bowls, although I'm not sure she was getting a goldfish to take home.

I don't think she would get booked for our local social club, although I can imagine the room would be pretty full if she was. Makes Paul Daniels and Debbie McGee look pretty pathetic. Personally I would like to see Mr and Mrs McGee on a desert island, preferably with no food. But with Paul's talent they wouldn't starve, they would have plenty of rabbits to eat. I didn't think I would ever be happy reading anything about Paul Daniels, but while we were catching up with the news from home we read that he had been assaulted by Sooty! What is the world coming to, has Sooty been playing too many violent computer games?

I remember as a kid seeing my mother stick a darning needle right through her breast. I thought it was a trick for years until I got older and realised she wore a padded bra. I thought she was an early Penn and Teller.

We left Bangkok in a taxi, not a tuk-tuk, and arrived at the railway station where we were looking forward to spending the next 13 hours on an overnight train. We were going to be sharing a cabin with two others and couldn't wait to get on board. It was the first time we had been on an overnight sleeper train. Tony was hoping for two tall slim Scandinavians who might ask him in slow, sexy voices to apply lotion to their sunburned backs. 'That is so gooood...' I was rather hoping for two black men on their way to a porn shoot who needed fluffing.

On the train, our hopes were dashed. We were not as we thought in a cabin with two others. The train had top and bottom bunks complete with numbered curtains. Under me (as it were) I had a very large man with a camp voice who could easily have been a really bad-looking ladyboy, or perhaps Ting Tong from Little Britain, and Tony had a six-stone Thai man under him, though even at that size he still looked menacing. I don't know what it is but you always expect someone with an oriental appearance to turn into Jackie Chan and start performing flying kicks and throwing star-shaped weapons at your forehead. Or is that just me?

I spotted the ladder I would have to climb to reach the top bunk, and I was slightly nervous, wondering what the weight restriction was - judging by the majority of the Thais, probably not too much. I could see the story in the Thai Gazette: 'FAT LASS KILLS STUDENT ON TRAIN... It took fire fighters six hours to free a Thai student from the wreckage of a collapsed bunk'.

We had been on board for about ten minutes when I spotted the first cockroach. It seemed to be waiting to scare the shit out of anyone in its path, which meant me, as the man who was sitting next to me had just brushed one off his leg. I was now actually pleased that I was on the top bunk and didn't give a shit whether I killed anyone or not.

I decided to order some fried rice from the menu, thinking surely it will be ok if it's only a portion of rice. About twenty minutes later it arrived. It looked good until the waitress reached under the seat and pulled a table out and I saw dozens of cockroaches scuttle back under the seats. Nothing I could do. I was on this train till morning, so best get used to it. Thankfully there were no cockroaches in my rice, which surprisingly I enjoyed.

We were wondering how the beds worked. If the person on the top bunk wanted to go to bed that would be OK, but the bottom bunk was the seating area for both people. We didn't wonder for very long, as the porter arrived to pull the top bunks out and make the beds up. It was only eight o'clock!

He pulled out the top bunk and got out the bedding. It was packed in plastic covers and immaculate, which was a relief. Then he did the bottom bunks. In answer to our query, you have no choice what time you go to bed, it's 8 pm whether you like it or not.

The train was exactly like you see on an old black and white movie or a Carry On film, very old and worn. It was the first time we had been on a sleeper train so we were quite excited. The curtains went the full length of the train and each curtain was numbered so when you return you know which your bunk is. We were peeping out of the curtains like Barbara Windsor and Sid James.

You could hear the snoring of the Thais already, and they had only been in bed for five minutes. They like their sleep. The train was very slow and you could feel every movement as it cut through fields and tiny towns consisting of about three houses. It was very basic and I think the speed was probably all it could muster.

The four rungs up to my bed were a doddle, but I wish I could say the same about the hole in the floor for the toilet. It's difficult squatting over a hole in the floor on a moving train, could be quite messy. Thank God I found an 'English' sitting-down toilet.

I had a great night's sleep, unlike Tony, who was scared to go to sleep in case he shat himself - what was he saying, 'eat everything, it's lovely'? Well he was shitting through the eye of a needle now. He had been trying to squat over the hole all night with his shorts in his hand above his head because I forgot to mention the proper sitting-down toilet.

Chapter Four

NORTHERN THAILAND
AND KO SAMET

8TH NOVEMBER 2010

We finally arrived in Chang Mai, north Thailand, population 174,000 (most of them cockroaches). We got off the train and were immediately mugged by drivers wanting to take us to our hostel. They lunged towards us trying to snatch our bag and pull us into their taxi, very in your face and quite scary as there are so many people and we nearly got separated.

After negotiating a good price and leaving them to fight it out among themselves we settled for a small taxi with a canny little driver who laughed all the time, could speak no English and had evidently also never seen a dentist. He could have eaten an apple through a letterbox. If the taxi business went a bit slow he could easily have been employed putting the pattern on pastry crusts.

He drove us to the outskirts of town, where we were staying at a place called the Banihila. There were cats everywhere, which suited me but not everyone, my brother would have had a fit. There are not a lot of tourists in this area and it's quite a strange place, not really the type of spot you want to be in if you're feeling a bit down, because there are lots of cockroaches and it's pretty dirty in parts.

I tried to order egg fried rice and got a bowl of boiled rice with a fried egg on the top. We walked around town and it was evident that we were in the minority when it came to tourists here. We got a bottle of beer each in a small roadside bar and the waitress poured it into the glass. We smiled and thanked her, but as soon as we had taken a mouthful she was back over to top it up again. This went on and on. At first it was OK, but then I wanted to say 'For fuck's sake leave my beer alone!

I tried to take a mouthful when she wasn't looking, but she spotted me and she came back. So we sat and drank our beer having it topped up every bloody two minutes and watching rats as big as cats running in and out of the nearby sewer. They ran into the road and picked up scraps of food, but no one seemed concerned. At least we had the peace of mind of knowing we had plenty of cats at our hostel, so the rats must be at a minimum. A crowd of young lads threw a can at one, and for a minute it looked like it was going to throw it back, I couldn't believe the size of it. But when we looked around at the waste food lying on the pavements it wasn't surprising.

A van appeared selling food and I looked to see what I could eat there, but all they had were fried locust, fried crickets, fried cockroaches and fried lizard. Somehow I lost my appetite. Give me a packet of salt and vinegar crisps any day.

We strolled into town, which took us about half an hour. On the way we passed many beautiful buildings and shrines to various people. We didn't know who any of them were, but they were obviously very important or dead, or both, judging by the number of flowers thrown on the statues.

It reminded me of the time when my mother's friend came home with a bunch of flowers. I said 'They're nice, where did you get them?' 'They were just lying on the side of the road, so I picked them up' she replied. So, sorry to whoever laid the flowers. There was no malice intended and if it's any consolation they did look lovely in a blue vase.

There was an event going on to do with the elephant. We tried to get some information, thinking it was to celebrate the elephant's life and how it has been used over the years in logging and various work before machinery took over and the animals were retired. Either way it was a very pretty spectacle with huge ornamental elephants in the town square. I was glad I wasn't wearing my flip-flops as the cockroaches were everywhere. Strange how I was dodging them and down the road they were being served up on plates.

9TH NOVEMBER

The next day we paid a visit to a place of sanctuary for orphaned tigers. They were gorgeous. Some are now bred in captivity though, and I'm not sure it's for the right reasons. I don't usually like this kind of thing, but after speaking to a lad who was staying at our hostel and worked in a Florida zoo we learned that the conditions for the tigers were excellent, so we paid a visit. We played with two six-month old cubs and they were gorgeous, jumping on us and licking my ear. I loved it.

After playing with the cubs I went into the swimming pool area, where a huge tiger was swimming and jumping in and out the pool. Tony pushed me into the enclosure, saying something about insurance under his breath, and said he would take the photos from the other side of the fence. The man with the tiger gave instructions on how to jump the electric fence if needed. I thought I would never be able to jump over it, until I got in and saw the size of the tiger. When it started coming towards me to 'play' I realised that yes, I could get over that fence if needed, in fact I think I could give Linford Christie a run for his money.

Thankfully the lad in charge diverted the tiger and it jumped back in the pool, soaking me along the way. It was a fantastic experience and worth the risk. You would never be able to experience anything like that in England.

11TH - 14TH NOVEMBER

We travelled with the local taxi driver to the bus station to go to Chang Rai. We were travelling again on the local bus and the journey was going to be about six hours. The bus was comfortable and not packed. There was a film showing in Thai, so no good for us, but we watched out of the windows all the way. Some of the places we passed were stunning and very pretty. We passed many people working in the rice fields knee deep in water. It's back-breaking work and the heat was incredible, more so because they were fully clothed and had their faces, legs and arms covered.

Chang Rai is Thailand's northernmost province, where the Mekong River runs through. This is another place where there are not many tourists. There are also no tuk-tuks here. It is a lovely little place where everyone speaks to you for no other reason than to be nice.

At first when an elderly gentleman said 'hello' we were suspicious and were on our guard, thinking 'What is he going to ask us for?', but we soon found that this is known as the friendliest place in northern Thailand. Not a lot of English is spoken here and I had to resort to Pictionary methods again to order food. For someone who got O level art I can't even draw a chicken now, so the only option is to flap my arms up and down while making a chicken sound. They laughed and I think they got the picture, because I got what I think was chicken.

We were staying at a hostel called the Mirror Art, which donates some of its profits to a foundation called the Mirror Art Foundation, set up to help the hill tribe people and to recruit voluntary workers to teach English/Skills to both adults and children. We read about the organisation and decided that we would like to know more. When we met one of the hill tribe people who spent a lot of his time at the foundation, we spoke to him and told him we wanted to go into the jungle if we could. He volunteered to take us. He had been brought up in a hill tribe called the Karib, so he knew the jungle very well, which we thought would come in pretty handy. His name was totally unpronounceable, so he told us to call him Karib, with emphasis on the K.

I thought this would be a laugh as Tony is hopeless at remembering names. Once while we were on holiday we met a lad called Dawson. Tony said 'How am I going to remember that?'

'Just think of the holiday company Dawson and Sanderson.'

The next morning Tony said 'Morning Wallace.'

Dawson laughed, and I said 'Where the hell did you get Wallace from'

'Wallace Arnold coach trip holidays.'

Karib was a nice little man, apart from the long black hairs on his chin which he constantly groomed. They were about four inches and had the consistency of thick twine, so I couldn't look at him without feeling ill. Every so often I would actually have to look at him otherwise it would seem rude, so I used to think 'please don't be touching it' and I would look and sure enough he was. Back to feeling ill.

He said we had to go and eat, because the trek was strenuous and we needed to take in some energy and fluids. We drove to a few places that were closed (I thanked the lord for this), but then he found one that was open, right in the middle of nowhere. It was a shelter made of bits of ply with a corrugated roof, and housed several gas bottles attached to a couple of woks. There were a few crudely-made tables and plastic chairs and lots of children, kittens, dogs, and chickens running around.

Our man spoke to the lady in Thai and she quickly picked up her machete. There was a chicken running around and I was terrified she was just going to decapitate it there and then. I think she knew what I was thinking by the look on my face, and she picked up a load of noodles and laughed as she threw them into a black, well-used wok.

We took off our shoes and went inside. It was a lovely little place, so basic but the hospitality was wonderful. The little kids came over to watch us eat and giggled at our attempts to speak Thai. They showed us their school work, and although I don't speak Thai I could make out that the little boy was getting into trouble for not taking off his school uniform - the world is not that different anywhere really.

I pointed at the noodles and the rice. Tony opted for a mixture of noodles, rice, chicken, pork, lamb and vegetables. She cooked it in front of us, frying and chopping with such professionalism. The food was very good, and we ate it with the children still giggling and laughing at us. She charged us the equivalent of about fifty pence for the three meals.

When we were finished the kids walked us to the Jeep and ran after us, blowing us kisses and waving as we drove off. We stopped after about half an hour and Karib told us that it was best if we took a boat upstream while he drove to meet us at the other end, as the terrain was pretty rough. (I did wonder if he had had enough of us already and was his way of getting rid of us.) He told us to keep our hands in the boat because of crocodiles - we still don't know if he was kidding or not. Either way I wasn't taking any chances.

Karib spoke to a little old man in a boat. He looked as if he could have been anything from fifty years old to a hundred, so I couldn't make out if the years had been good to him or not. What was more frightening was that it looked as if he had made the little boat himself. The next thing we knew we were being helped into the boat and sat down. Once we were comfortable he started his engine and away we went upstream.

For about two hours we were passing little fishing boats and people waving to us from the banks. We then reached a place where we had to transfer to another form of transport - an elephant. We had to climb up a roughly-made platform and climb on to the elephant, which had a double seat on its back, the most uncomfortable thing I have ever sat on in my life. For about half an hour, the poor elephant heaved and bumped into everything in its path and I didn't like it one bit, I felt so sorry for him. I bet he had thought that when his logging days were over he would be able to relax and eat bananas, but instead he had ended up carrying fat people around the jungle. I would have rather walked and taken my chances.

A short while later we got off the elephant. We were glad as it looked knackered. We then heard a gunshot and thought the elephant had had to be shot! We looked at each other and were horrified, but thankfully later we heard it had made a full recovery!

Tony had now realised that he had lost his watch, the one he had said wasn't too tight. He had also taken a load of shit photos!

We trekked through some fantastic parts of the jungle, where we were reminded to watch for snakes and monkeys. We climbed and climbed until eventually we saw the most amazing view. We looked down and saw lots of people working in the field. Karib told us they were cutting corn, but as the temperature was in the high thirties it looked such hard work.

We started our walk down, with plenty stops for water and rest. We asked Karib if we could watch them, and he went off and spoke to the group. A man from the group immediately offered us his machete and gestured for us to get to work, while the rest laughed as he sat down to watch us. They were in good humour and we were made to feel welcome.

After a quick demonstration that lasted about two minutes (they didn't bother with the health and safety lecture), we were put to the test. Tony nearly lost his pride, along with a few other things, when he swished the machete a bit too near his groin. But at least his watch wasn't going to fly off now.

We stopped after a short time because we were knackered. I hoped they hadn't been expecting an early finish when Friday came around, because we had only cleared an area the size of a double quilt and they still had several fields to cut. We were wearing cropped pants and vests and they were wearing long sleeved tops with long trousers and a hat and scarf covering their full face - they don't like to be tanned as it is a reflection of their class. A tan shows they work in low-paid jobs, usually outside in the fields or selling on the streets. We idiots walk around with our cream on actively encouraging the sun to change the colour of our skin.

Off we went up to the hill tribe village, which was a massive trek especially as the heat was in the thirties. Karib, who weighed about six stone, was like a mountain goat (complete with hideous beard), and he had done this trek a million times. He walked in front, kicking snakes and whatever else was lurking in our path, and generally telling us where not to walk. Several times we stopped to take some beautiful photographs and enjoyed the opportunity to get a breather.

We came to a large clearing and saw that it was the pathway into a small village. We passed chickens, hens, cockerels, goats, cats, dogs and then loads of kids on the way up. The kids spotted us and started running towards us with their hands outstretched in a gesture of greeting. They surprised us by being able to speak a few words of English. They were all barefoot and had scruffy little faces, and they were all gorgeous.

A lady who was the mother of several of the kids that were following us invited us into her house. Access was by a small ladder like the ones you see on bunk beds, and I was worried that it wouldn't take our weight. She only looked about twenty herself and had five small kids, one of which was a baby in a sling thrown around her neck and shoulder. It was incredible on two counts, one that we didn't go through the floor and the other was the sight we saw once inside.

There was only one big room with about nine kids all sitting round watching a little coloured portable television, all glued to a Kung Fu film. There were mats to sleep on and a home-made wardrobe with little school uniforms hanging up.

Karib was speaking to one of the mothers, who told us that the kids walked every day together for an hour and a half to and from school in the local village where we had just left - a pretty hard trek. They ate rice for their breakfast and again for lunch, and their evening meal was usually chicken, again with rice.

The children were all smiling and giggling under their hands. They were laughing and offering us food and a place to stay the night, patting the double mattress that lay on the floor. One little boy of about eight gave me a piece of tomato with lots of spices on and watched while I ate it - it was delicious. Karib told me the spices were grown by the family and sold.

They grabbed my hand to show me around their village. There was a small and very basic toilet block which some volunteers had built a year previously, and they loved to show their appreciation. I loved the experience and was genuinely moved with emotion. It made me think that our Western world has not quite got it right. You could ask yourself 'Who is really the richest'? It was one of the most beautiful experiences I have ever encountered in my entire life and I will never forget it.

Until our last night at the hostel I luckily hadn't seen the cockroaches. I was sitting on the bed when out of the corner of my eye I noticed something move and saw three huge cockroaches running across the floor. Tony managed to get one with his flip-flop, while the other two ran out of the door on to the grass outside. When I got up in the night to go to the bathroom I opened the door very slowly. I was expecting to see a load of cockroaches in the bathroom but I didn't. I stood for a while to make sure that it was clear to go in, and just as I was about to step in a huge one ran out from under the door. Tony was awoken by my blood curdling scream, as was the rest of the hostel I think. As he jumped out of bed expecting to find me being murdered, he banged his foot on the cabinet. By the look on his face I didn't know who he was going to kill first, the cockroach or me. Thankfully it was nearly time to get up anyway, because from then on every time the sheet moved I thought it was a cockroach. They say they are the only things that will survive a nuclear attack. I was thinking of collecting my bags of pasta and water in case of an attack, but I don't think I will bother now.

In the early hours in the morning we jumped in a taxi to the airport to fly back to Bangkok.

15TH NOVEMBER-19TH NOVEMBER

We arrived at Bangkok Airport and searched for the bus stand to travel to Pattaya. Eventually we found it, but we had to wait an hour. A bit of pushing and shoving ensued, and then we were on our way.

There were some interesting characters on our bus. It appeared that all the young Thai girls have European 'granddads'! One man looked over sixty and the Thai girl who was with him was telling him she loved him. She was very convincing!

We were staying in the area of Jomtien Beach, which is a massive place full of bars, restaurants, tourist shops and Russians. There is a very large sex tourist trade here and the infamous 'Walking Street', the most famous street in Thailand for sex workers, is only a short distance away. We had found a lovely hostel and had a room on the fifth floor, where you can rent the room by the hour. You would have to be pretty naive to wonder why anyone would only want to stay for an hour!

Overall the place was immaculate. In our room we found a bottle of lovemaking enhancers which the last occupants had obviously left. It had been left on top of the wardrobe, but I spotted it on coming out of the bathroom. The Thais are mostly not very tall, and it could have quite easily have been missed by a three-foot high cleaner. We handed it back to the owner/manager, a French bloke who had been married to a Thai lady for the last twenty years. He was mortified but he put it straight into his back pocket. I was so relieved that he spoke English, because it could have quite easily been misinterpreted as an invitation to come to our room.

I was crippled with stomach pains and shitting and vomiting, so we had to extend our stay. The manager was concerned and told Tony what to get me from the chemist, which thankfully was not from his back pocket. My impression of a chicken might not have got me a chicken after all.

17TH NOVEMBER

After loads of water and 16 hours' sleep, I felt much better and felt I could risk a day at the beach. Tony thought the beach was nice. In fact the part where we were was a dive, but I couldn't be bothered to go in search of a nice spot for fear my stomach cramp returned and filled my new polka dot bikini.

After telling two ladies for the tenth time that we didn't want a massage, they still kept coming back with their oils. Tony had pretended to be asleep, but she had started to massage his feet, much to his annoyance. A quick kick and she was gone. A green and yellow hairy caterpillar fell on me from the tree, so that shifted me. It had also bitten me. I showed the deckchair attendant and he recalled in horror and threw me a tub of cream to rub on. I was thinking I would wake up breathing like Darth Vader and looking like John Merrick, the Elephant Man

When I woke up there was no swelling from my bite. I did feel like John Merrick, but I think that was down to the Chang Lager. If they sold Chang in our club it would be bankrupt within a week, because you only need three bottles to lose two days. It's like anaesthetic in a bottle. You know you drank it but you can't remember a thing. It's like legalised Rohypnol.

18TH NOVEMBER

One night we paid a visit to the Walking Street, which featured on the television series 'big trouble in little Thailand'. We were approached by many young men offering us the opportunity to see shows and buy girls or boys. Some of the women we saw should have been relegated to the top floor, and their advertisement should read 'customers to bring their own ladder'! I don't know how they make money. We spoke to one of the volunteer tourist police, who told us that the girls had to be a minimum of eighteen to work on the street. I had great difficulty in believing that they all complied, after seeing some of the young females on offer. We didn't stay long after practically being dragged into a 'free show', as we know there is nothing free in Thailand. This is probably the seediest place I have ever visited in my life.

19TH NOVEMBER

The next day we caught the public bus to the island of Ko Samet. The bus was fitted with air con and had huge windows. We were looking forward to seeing how beautiful Ko Samet was, as everyone raves about it.

We arrived at the ferry terminal for the 90-minute crossing, and found the ferry a lot bigger than we had expected. We all piled on.

The crossing was lovely with crystal-clear blue water, and the spray of the sea from the boat was warm. It was brilliant, apart from the fact that there were about two hundred people on board and the life jacket box was the size of a large cornflakes packet!

We all sat in the boat on little wooden bench seats and felt the breeze run through our hair. The temperature was red hot but it felt cool due to the boat moving through the waves. There wasn't much on board except passengers and a few twelve-year-old crew members.

We soon saw Ko Samet coming into sight. On arrival we were helped off the ferry by the crew members, who looked about 14. We then had to leap a gap of about a metre on to the pier, where we collected our rucksacks, which were being thrown off quicker than we could get on. I think they needed to fill the boat up to get people back across. We didn't hear any splashes, so I assumed everyone made it.

My first impressions of Ko Samet were total shock. It is a National Park, yet the boatyard and the main street to the beach were anything but beautiful, and the streets were littered with stray dogs and rubbish.

I heard a conversation between a little girl and her nanna:

'Oh Nanna, look at the big dog, what's it doing?'

'Oh, they're just playing, that's all'

'But someone's glued them together, Nanna.'

'Well, because that's what dogs do.'

'Yes, but they're glued together, Nanna he's trying to get away!'

'Look out for your Mum, she said she would meet us here.'

I admired the grandmother's efforts, but from where I'm standing it looked to me like Rex had successfully managed to glue himself to poor little Lassie underneath and was having his wicked way whether Lassie liked it or not.

The Nanna spotted her daughter, and thankfully Rex was left to take advantage of Lassie without any witnesses. We walked from the ferry area on to the main street to find that every other shop was a moped repair garage, which says a lot about the number of accidents involving mopeds. We saw a sign that we recognised from our directions and followed it uphill. We were staying at a hostel up a hill where a lot of local people live, as it was a lot cheaper than staying near the beach (which was only a ten minute stroll anyway) and that's in flip-flops.

It was very friendly where we were staying - not very scenic in the tourist sense, but we loved it because it was the picture of local life. Our street was like the local factory units. There were people on sewing machines inside little shacks, while other little shacks were turning out the most amazing leather moped seats and leather chairs.

One night we were sitting on the veranda of our hostel and watched the family opposite clear their mattresses and pieces of furniture to one side of the room so that they could cover the floor in leather in order to cut the patterns out to be stitched. They literally lived, worked and slept in that one room. After the first night it became evident that these small shacks were turning out the most incredible merchandise and operating right into the night to get the orders out.

Because we were up on a hill there was a big problem with the drainage system. After three nights our room smelt like a men's urinal and the water from the shower was not draining away, so we just about had trench foot. For fear of contracting some terrible disease I went off to the beach and looked around. I looked at some of the beach huts for rent, and found some of them were only a couple of quid a night. For that you literally got a wooden room with a mattress on the floor and a mosquito net. I thought I would rather pay the extra few quid and have a decent room.

I found us a new hostel a five-minute walk from the beach, so we made our way back to get our bags and checked out. We had to invest in a torch, because in the evening we had to cut through a small forest area to get back and at night it was pitch black. We got back to our hostel and didn't mention our trench foot problem - we just said we wanted to be closer to the beach and headed off.

We walked along the main street towards the beaches. If your accommodation is on the beach you have to pay a park fee, otherwise you can visit the beach for free. I think this was a rip off. The guards obviously know who is going on to stay because of their luggage, but I told Tony to keep on walking and hoped the fat security guard would not approach us. My plan worked. He couldn't be bothered and stayed in his wooden hut eating noodles.

We got a lovely new room at a place called the Lelawadee, where we negotiated a deal to stay seven nights and saved the equivalent of about £4 each.

We decided to chill for a while on the beach before we moved on to somewhere else. It was very nice having only the two of us and a big lizard sharing the room. I didn't mind the lizard - I was hoping he would eat the mosquitoes. It was well worth the move and the walk, because the beach was beautiful, clear blue sea and gorgeous sand. There was one small café with a few beach huts.

We met an older couple from Austria who basically invited themselves to sit with us. He was 75 and she was 72. They had been travelling to Ko Samet for the past 30 years and were one of the first 'tourists' on the island before there was electricity. Considering that there are on average five power cuts a day it's scary to think what it would have been like before the 10-watt bulbs they now use were introduced.

They were quite an inspirational couple. They swam around the island with their waterproof backpacks. He said it was not as easy now and I assumed he was talking about their age, but he then told me it was because of the increase in boats and jet skis. We talked about our favourite city breaks, and I said our trip to Poland to visit

Auschwitz had been a very moving experience. That's when Tony kicked me in the shin.

At night we phoned my brother James on Skype with Jackie, and Ronnie and Reggie (aka Jack and Ben). It was brilliant to see them, especially when they told us that the weather was cold, wet and miserable at home. We also used Skype to speak for about ten minutes to one of my mother's eyebrows. She simply does not understand the concept of appearing in the little box. She even said she had stopped smoking, when we could blatantly see the cigarette in her mouth!

We spent a day jumping off the pier, eating pineapples and swinging on a swing on the beach. Life doesn't get much better than that.

We ate tea on the beach and met a nice lad called Eddy from Norwich, who Tony kept calling Tom. We watched some Mau Thai boxing, which prompted Tony to tell me more stories from his skinhead fighting days. It sounded as if he had fought everyone from the Byker Boot boys to the Triads, who he says both ran away.

We found a small bar on the beach with very little other than a few plastic tables and chairs and cheap beer, but they also had a television where we watched a game – Newcastle 1, Chelsea 1.

Tony had the same ritual every time we left the room. I would say 'I've got the camera and the key and stuff' then we would leave the room and start walking. Two minutes down the road he would pat his pockets and say 'I've forgotten the camera'. 'I've got it Tony', I'd reply. Then another two minutes down the road he'd say 'I've forgotten the mosquito stuff'. 'I've got it Tony'. Two more minutes and he'd say 'I've...' I would say 'Don't even go there. I've got the camera, the mosquito stuff, the key, the torch, so don't mention one more thing' He then rolls his eyes and says 'eh, your temper!' I would smile through gritted teeth. One month and 39 domestics done!

We left Ko Samet after 11 days of sheer bliss and made our way back by local bus to Bangkok. On the way I struck up a conversation with two young lads who were Thai and quite evidently a gay couple. I was attempting to ask them if they had been staying on the island or if they had been for the day, so I put my hands together and put them up to my ear to make out like I was sleeping. Unfortunately it looked as if I was asking them if they slept together, and it was getting worse as I tried to dig myself out. When the bus came I noticed they sat at the back away from me.

30TH NOVEMBER

After a few hours on the bus we arrived back at Bangkok, where we were booked into a hotel near the airport called the Sanawan Palace, recommended to us by the Austrian couple we had met in Ko Samet. They had given us a card and we wrote the directions down and showed it to the bus driver in the hope that he would drop us off nearby, as the bus was passing very close. He remembered to stop and let us off, and we walked for about ten minutes to a little taxi rank and got a cab. It was a shame we were only at the Sanawan for one night as it was cheap and spot on. It had a gorgeous pool and food menu, and was owned and run by a bloke from Whitby. He even did his own version of Whitby fish and chips. We had to be up at 4 am for the airport to fly to Vietnam.

Chapter Five

VIETNAM

We left the hotel and travelled back to the airport by taxi – the taxis were so cheap that there was no point in taking the local bus. We checked in our bags and headed to the bar. I'm not a great lover of Heineken lager but it was better than the other choice, which was Chang.

After a few hours flight we arrived in Hanoi, Vietnam. It was sweltering hot and there were lots of people milling around. Before we could leave the airport we had to go to immigration and get our visas. We had already done the paperwork in England and applied on line, so it cut down the process a bit - there was a big queue of people waiting. I had to apply for mine twice, as Tony had forgotten to put my surname on the first one and if it's not spot on they won't allow you entry. The process is pretty quick - unless you are American that is, then for some reason you have to wait ages!

We were shown into a area with a large counter, and names were shouted one by one. There was no particular order, just a lot of luck that whoever is doing your visa can work pretty quickly.

In the queue we met an American who had served in Vietnam and had lost a few of his friends there. He was one of the many Americans who return to 'lay a few ghosts to rest' in what was in our opinion a totally pointless war. Tony's name was pretty quick and his visa was sorted, but we waited a while longer for mine. I was aware that a lady was shouting something, but didn't know what at first. It wasn't until I realised that no one else seemed to be doing anything other than looking around that I realised that she was actually shouting my name. It sounded nothing like my name, but it was my passport in her hand and my visa was complete, so off we went.

The hostel we were staying in had sent a free taxi to pick us up. You do have to be careful with this as one of the scams, is that the driver will take you to a hostel that is not the one you are booked into but has the same name. We had a reference number from the hostel when we booked on line, so we ended up at the correct place. We were staying at the Little Hanoi hostel, which was a lovely place with free breakfast and free internet access.

We were greeted by a lovely lady who gave us hot tea and French bread. We thought this was probably a sweetener because we hadn't seen the room yet, but we were wrong and the room was excellent.

We ventured out of the hostel to have a good look around and quickly learned that the traffic here is horrendous. The roads were mental. There are literally hundreds of mopeds coming at you from each direction. The policy is that you walk out and the traffic, which is mainly mopeds, goes around you. Don't run or stop, and they'll negotiate their way around you. Imagine doing that on a busy road in England. It's easier said than done, because after 20 minutes we were still plucking up the courage to step out. We had been sweating with fear since we decided to cross.

Tony went first and I watched in anticipation from the kerb. It actually looked quite easy, but putting it into practice was another matter. I had to cross now as Tony was now on the other side of the road laughing at me, so I counted to ten a few times in my head, then stepped out. I took my time, but I got across without any mishaps or broken bones.

Another way is to tuck in behind one of the locals and go with them. Once you have done it you feel great, and find yourself showing off by stepping out in front of the obvious new people, rather like when you're on holiday and the first few days you're finding your feet. When you see people on first name terms with the barman, you think 'tosser', but after a few days you're on first name terms yourself and you look like the tosser.

Hanoi is an incredible place, loads to see - if you can cross the roads. They have streets named after what is sold on them, for example Sunglasses Street, a whole street of shops selling sunglasses, then Paint Street, Clothes Street, Coffin Street, even Dog Street - but we didn't go there. It would be too upsetting, as they definitely weren't pet shops!

Up early after a great night's sleep and we went off to see Ho Chi Minh at the Mausoleum where he lies in state. The Mausoleum is situated in the historic Ba Dinh square where Ho Chi Minh read the declaration of independence on 2nd September 1945. We were extremely lucky as we were informed that he had only just returned from Russia where he is apparently taken every year to be 'worked on' (not sure what the process is, but he looks good). We stood in the queue and everyone was reminded to be silent, to remove hats, remove hands from pockets and not to take any photographs. It's all very respectful. Inside the Mausoleum, which is an architectural work of great political and ideological significance, expressing the profound feelings of the entire Vietnamese people, lies the man who is endearingly called Uncle Ho.

Inside it was very cold, thanks to the air conditioning, and it is only open for a few hours each day. We all walked along a marble hallway which took us down to the actual mausoleum area where Ho lay in state. He was in an open coffin, and not behind glass as I was expecting. We thought he looked like our mate Jimmy Herron, except that Jimmy's not dead.

Many of the visitors were Vietnamese, and they showed deep respect and profound feelings for the man who is honoured for his role as the liberator of the Vietnamese people from colonialism, as much as his communist ideology. This is reinforced by the education system in Vietnam, which emphasises Ho Chi Minh's deeds and accomplishments.

The mausoleum was guarded by white uniformed guards. It was very beautiful and peaceful. Clearly Ho was a very inspiring man who the Vietnamese people adored and respected.

3RD DECEMBER

There are loads of places in Hanoi that offer the trip to Halong Bay, but we opted for the one being run by our hostel. We checked it out then booked it. The bay is one of the unofficial wonders of the world. We caught the bus which was part of the trip and found it was being driven by a driver who possibly gave Lewis Hamilton lessons. We arrived at the terminal after four hours and boarded the boat along with eight other people. We would be sleeping on board that night as we sailed Halong Bay. The boat was fantastic and the journey out to sea was breathtakingly beautiful. We had a school of dolphins swim with us. The scenery was amazing and we saw many extremely well-maintained boats on the sea.

Off the dining area was a large highly-varnished wooden door which once opened revealed our room. This contained a bed with a large window at its foot. It also had an en-suite shower room. It was lovely to be able to lie on the bed and watch the bay and the views, though we hadn't been long on the journey when we spotted the first rat lurking down on deck. It ran out and appeared to have a good look around before scuttling back to wherever it had come from. We were now miles out to sea, so it was certainly travelling with us. We couldn't go anywhere, so we had to get used to it. Each time I went into our room I made as much noise as possible in case it was there. We didn't see any in our room but we did hear the odd noise through the night, and in the morning half the Pringles had been taken from our box, while the ones that were left all had nibbled edges.

We passed a 'floating village' where 400 people lived on what looked like little floating sheds. They made their money from the sea, and it's pretty incredible to witness this. What an amazing existence. Some of them even had a dog the poor thing can't have got get many walks, and it only had a small platform to walk around.

The staff served us dinner, and to our surprise it wasn't fried rat! The meal was excellent, apart from a fish that lay staring at me throughout the meal - at one point I could have sworn I saw it blink. It looked as if it was going to burst into Shake, Rattle and Roll like Billy the Bass, the electronic singing fish that was popular a few years back. It would have been an improvement on the Vietnamese karaoke.

When we sat out on deck at night, little rowing boats from the floating village appeared, selling various items from crisps and nibbles to alcohol. One of the girls on board tried to pull a fast one. Instead of buying her booze on the boat (which is as cheap as chips) she bought a bottle of wine from the seller. She took pride in letting everyone know that she was not paying the price on board when she could buy it herself cheaper (it's about a quid a bottle on board and about fifty pence off the seller). They were still on the sea in the early hours in the morning and would row from boat to boat. Eventually we heard in the pitch black distance the voice of a woman singing. It was quite eerie at first, then funny as we realised that she was probably quite drunk and on her home after a good night's trading. We thought how easily she could disappear into the blackness of the sea, with only a tiny torch for a light.

The next day, after a good night's sleep, we visited the biggest cave

I have ever seen in my life. You could have got a shopping centre into in, it was massive. It was like something from an Indiana Jones movie.

We got off the boat and into a kayak, which I absolutely hated. We rowed around getting soaked with Tony saying 'Oh look at this' and 'Oh look at that'. I hated every minute of it and at every opportunity I got I soaked him with my oar. Give me a jet ski any day of the week.

When it was time to get off the boat we all had to settle our tabs. We owed a few quid for beers, along with most people, and the girl who bought the wine got charged for corkage!

From the 1st till the 15th December each year the Vietnamese eat a lot of dogmeat. They actually eat dog all year round, but they believe that at this time eating the flesh of the dog brings them good luck and any problems they are experiencing will disappear. Try telling that to Tyson when he's just brought your slippers. 'Now Tyson, thanks for my slippers but you know I've had a lot on my mind lately…'

On the journey back, driving through the city, we saw a basket full of little dogs on the back of a moped, all trying to get out. Their little paws and faces were sticking through the netting. It broke my heart. I wanted to push the moped driver off and capture them, a bit like Cruella De Vil in 101 Dalmatians, but without wanting the coat.

Apart from that upsetting experience, the journey back was very interesting. We cut through the outskirts of town and got back to the hostel courtesy of a driver who drove like Sebastian Vettel. When we got back the hostel had given our room away, but when we explained that we had actually booked and paid a deposit for the room they got the message. They apologised and explained that the hostel was now fully booked but they were going to transfer us to a hotel which was a lot more expensive, but because it was their fault they were going to pay. They even sent a taxi for us. We were transferred to the King Ly Hotel, which was lovely. Thank God for mistakes.

There is a huge lake in Hanoi which is the central focus of the town, where people spend the day on the many bench seats around the lake. It is very popular with weddings, and a lot of couples have their photos taken here. It's a strange idea - they do their photos either weeks beforehand or after the actual wedding day, so you will see sometimes more than 40 brides and grooms being photographed. I imagined Tony taking the pictures, no feet, no heads, the bride complaining 'I wasn't ready', Tony saying 'point and shoot love, point and shoot'. He would be in and out of court more often than a judge. I remember reading some 'wedding advice' for a Caribbean wedding in a magazine once and thought how different cultures are. A couple of paragraphs went something like this:

1. When you have lots of babies and the children are driving you mad you have to laugh at the children and hug your wife.

2. When your wife cooks you a meal, just eat the meal and never say you don't like her cooking.

3. You, the man, have to go to work and the wife must look after the home and the children. You must then go for drinks with the men after work and the wife must never ever complain.

I thought I would rewrite them, so here are mine:

1. Do not have any children. They are horrible little people who will only manage to wreck your home with dirty finger marks and chocolate on the furniture. Everyone believes that their baby is beautiful, when in actual fact they are all incredibly ugly. You will never be able to get a baby sitter, your vagina will become slack and your breasts will go south.

2. Ladies, if you do cook make sure he eats it, otherwise he can cook his own, after all he's a big boy now and if he can go to the pub on his own he can make his own tea.

3. If you have no kids you don't have to stay at home and watch little Damien, so when he goes out with his mates make sure you do the same.

4. If he is untidy, tell him. If he continues to be untidy, then leave him and find someone who is tidy and clean.

Just to let you all know that these were not my wedding vows, just some of the ones I agree with. Also at this point I would like to apologise to the vicar who asked me 'What do you like to see in a man, Stephanie?' When I said 'a knife' I was only joking.

We decided to visit Hoa Lo Prison, the Hanoi 'Hilton', and it was very interesting. There were some horrendous torture instruments. There again I don't suppose there's such a thing as a good torture instrument, unless perhaps you're a masochist. And I couldn't stand the pain, not after the last time!

A huge number of people wear face masks in Vietnam because of the pollution, which is mainly from the hundreds of mopeds on the street and from the local pavement stalls cooking food. Because of the pollution there is a lot of spitting which takes a bit of getting used to. You're just about to take a bite out of your sandwich when a great big green gob lands at your feet. I was worried I might contract TB. Brilliant if you're trying to lose weight, because you can't eat a thing at times. You try not to look, but I always do, and then I could kick myself.

In Hanoi the men and women gather on the street and sit on tiny plastic stools, or squat down and drink a local brew which is incredibly cheap and evidently, after watching them, very potent. Anyone can join them - it's basically their local pub but much cheaper, and you don't have to go outside to smoke. Not that I smoke. God knows what they do for the toilet, but judging by the state of some of their trousers it's not that much of an issue. Let's just say there are a few rusty zips around!

We pulled up a couple of chairs, which were the size of the ones you see in nursery schools, and the lady who was evidently acting as barmaid gave us two tiny glasses filled with a cream-coloured liquid.

We said thank you and she hovered over us smiling and showing the black insides of her mouth. The little fellas who were sitting around raised their glasses to us to say cheers. They too had black teeth and mouths, but we drank it anyway because we didn't want to appear rude. We just hoped we weren't going to wake up with black teeth and gums.

You could feel it hit the back of your throat - it nearly blew our heads off.. It was like a cross between engine oil and diesel, so we never really knew how it was brewed, but we staggered off light-headed after only one glass.

6TH DECEMBER

We travelled to Hue (pronounced hway) on an overnight sleeper bus for 14 hours and paid about seven quid each for the privilege. We were both on the top bunk again, which we were very pleased about. Once you're up its OK because on the bottom bunks at times you have the Vietnamese who have paid for the 'cheap travel', which basically means lying on the floor in the aisle. If I need the toilet in the night a few of them could be crushed under foot!

Your legs are already fully stretched in the seat, so all you do is recline your seat and it becomes a bed, practically flat. If they did this on flights it would be excellent. It goes back a lot more than four inches. You get a blanket and a pillow and the waitress comes with duty free. No, I made the last bit up.

Tony was lying flat on his back with the straps over him looking a bit like the bloke in One flew over the cuckoo's nest before he was wheeled off for his frontal lobotomy. I couldn't stop laughing, but this way of travel is incredibly comfortable.

About eight hours into our journey we were awoken by the sound of screaming and nearly died, thinking the bus was going to crash or the driver was on a suicide mission. I think the driver had passed his Formula One test, so I wasn't too worried about him crashing. The screaming was coming from a man at the front who was having a nightmare. People around him were trying to calm him down. I couldn't help but think to myself, why don't you just open the door and push him out. He was causing a panic and I had been fast asleep.

We arrived in Hue to find it's a very quaint little place, only 500 mopeds coming at you altogether, instead of 500 from each direction! Our road crossing skills were now down to a fine art, or as Tony says it was a piece of piss. We were staying at the Tran-Ly Hotel, which was very nice. We were approached by about 30 taxi drivers all wanting to take us to the hostel, but we knew all the scams by now and politely told them we had a car coming. Muttering 'sod off' under our breath, we sat down with a smug look on our faces as if to say 'you can't catch us out with that old chestnut'.

Twenty minutes later we were still waiting for our lift to arrive and still being watched by the 30 taxi drivers who were sitting chatting (I'm sure about us) and waiting for the next bus to pull in. We now realised that our 'lift' was not coming, so we had to go over while eating a very large slice of humble pie and ask one of them very nicely if he would take us to the hostel. They had good cause to laugh at us.

7TH DECEMBER

Today we visited the Buddhist tombs, the Minh Mang Tomb, which was fantastic, the best so far, and the Tu Duc Tomb.

The Buddhist religion is based on a circle.
The beginning of life is in the human form.
The second stage of life is that of an animal.
The third stage is that of a spirit.

They say happiness is never in front of you and you have to search for it. They say that all happiness is in memories of something you have done already. (Which if you think about it is true, because the things you want you don't know will make you happy until they do, but when something makes you happy you remember it.)

They believe that this circle rotates forever, unless you achieve the perfect life in which you never kill any living being or eat any living creature or animal and are good and kind to your fellow man. If you achieve this, then at death your body can be cremated, as there is no need to return to earth and the circle becomes complete.

They say happiness is never in front of you, but it's often in front of me in the shape of a pint.

8TH DEC-12TH DEC

We set off on a 4

Four hour bus journey to Hoi An, where we were well and truly wedged in. They piled the rucksacks in the aisles, so if you wanted off it was tough! (It's like having a private booth on the bus). It was scary to think that you wouldn't be able to get off if there was an accident, but it's probably best not to think about that.

After quite a bumpy ride across some of the worst roads in Vietnam we arrived at the bus terminal (without accident). It took quite a while to offload the rucksacks before we could see the aisle again. It felt like someone had opened a door and let us out.

We had booked into the Greenfields Hostel. They had crap reviews last year because of an insect infestation, but we figured now it would be immaculate because they wouldn't want any more complaints. Our risk paid off and we were treated like royalty and given a fantastic room.

There are orphanages which tourists can visit, and one afternoon while we were sitting in a café we saw three Italian couples with a brand new baby each. We didn't find out how they had come by them, but we heard from others that it is a meeting place for new 'mothers' with their adopted babies. There is also a unit for the underprivileged, in particular those who suffer mental health problems. The mental health centre reminded me of when I was working in Custody, when a male prisoner was brought in with his care worker. He was a resident on a secure unit and the night before had watched a video of *The Matrix*. He decided to cut the back out of the leather settee to make a cape - now I know you shouldn't laugh but you do. It proves the point I suppose that television does contribute to what some people will do. Some will say not, but all little boys wanted to be the Lone Ranger and ride Trigger and would practise saying 'Kemosabe', while teenage girls on the other hand wanted to be one of Charlie's Angels. I suppose even back then I knew I was different, because I wanted to be Googie Withers, the governess from the TV show *Within These Walls*.

Hoi An is probably the best place in Vietnam for tailors and dress making shops; you can have a suit or anything else made. You can take a picture out of a catalogue, even design your own pair of shoes, and they will make them for you, it's incredible.

We went for the off-the-peg vests and Tony got charged more for having too many XXX's on the label. More material, they kindly pointed out while patting his stomach.

10TH DECEMBER

We paid a visit to An Hoi Island, where Tony found the cheapest beer so far. 4000 Vietnamese dong a glass and you get 30,000 to the pound. I'm no Carol Vorderman - you do the maths.

After the fiasco of the XXX's on Tony's T shirts we decided to hire bikes and cycle to the beach. It was nice sand and clear water, but we got pestered by sellers and when Tony refused to buy a bottle of sun cream she shouted to him 'Go fuck yourself!'. She had obviously had quite a stressful day and could probably do with a weekend in Blackpool with the lasses.

One of the girls who worked in the hostel was having a birthday party and kindly invited Tony and me. We went because we thought it would be rude not to, and we thought there would be free beer. It turned out that there was no beer, and the buffet consisted of chopped apples and fruit, salad, chopped mangoes, loads of poppadoms with fresh coriander, and birthday cake with lashings of lemonade and cola. We had a lovely time!

11TH DECEMBER

It was a scorching red hot day today, so I bought a sun block for my lips. I put loads on and kept applying it, for there is nothing worse than burning your mouth. A few hours later when we were in a beach bar I caught sight of myself in the mirror. I was mortified. I spat my Coke out in shock and looked at my face again. My mouth was bright red all the way from under my nose to the bottom of my chin. I looked as if I had just stepped out of the Billy Smart salon. I could have stood on the beach singing 'I've written a letter to daddy' like a scene from Whatever Happened to Baby Jane - either that or worn the back of the settee as a cape and got booked into the mental health unit. Tony said he hadn't noticed. Never again will I buy a sun block that changes colour with the sun.

Tonight we spoke to my mother on Skype, and this time we spoke to two eyebrows. I had sent her a couple of photos via her next door neighbour's email. I asked her if she had got the photographs and she said she had. She said 'The photo of you coming out of the sea reminded me of Angela Andrex when she was in Doctor Who.'

'You mean Ursula Andress in Doctor No' I said.

'That's what I said' she said.

Those of you who heard about the fiasco on the electric scooter in Asda would not be surprised at all.

12TH DECEMBER

We were up early in the morning and caught the bus to Quy Nohn (pronounced 'way none'). We travelled first class, by which I mean first class cattle truck. The bus stopped at various places including bus stops and shop doorways, and people even got on and off at the edges of fields where there was literally nothing else around for miles. We learned that 'direct' actually meant the direct route, not 'without stopping'. Every time it stopped the street sellers offered their wares through the open windows. They were selling baby chicks which had been plucked, then deep fried. They didn't look too appetizing to me and they still had their tiny little faces and beaks on, but they were going like hot cakes.

After what seemed like a hundred stops we finally arrived. Not a lot of tourists stop off here and it was clear from the way they were circling around us when we got off the bus that they were feeling my shaved head. They were all friendly enough though, although the lady with the machete and blood on her blouse looked a bit menacing. I was glad she had a meat stall as I was getting seriously worried.

We were looking around for anyone else who looked vaguely European, but saw no one. We ventured into what looked like a little café and shop and tried to order a cup of tea, but we were given a cup with coloured water with sticks and pebbles in it. It wasn't exactly PG Tips, but we smiled and paid up and made a mental note not to order the tea there again.

Tony ordered the chicken and when it arrived it had the biggest bone you have ever seen. No way could a chicken have a bone that size. Perhaps it was a road runner.

We booked in at the Binh Duong Hostel, which was lovely and enormous. It was apparently fantastic in its heyday, but unfortunately it was now in need of a good clean and a major facelift. I think the cleaning had been done by Stevie Wonder. However we had a balcony overlooking the beach, which more than made up for the cleaning.

After a cursory check of the bed for bugs and cockroaches, it was found to be clean, so that was enough for me. The beach stretched for miles in both directions and there was not one person on it - now that's what I call secluded. It was absolutely beautiful, totally unspoiled and natural, a real picture postcard scene.

When you looked out in the evening you could see the sea shining with shoals of luminous squid. It looked lovely. As there weren't many tourists here we ventured out with extra vigilance. At one point we came across about 20 young lads in army clothes all sitting around on the pavement. At first it was slightly intimidating as they were shouting at us, but we couldn't make out what they were saying. I heard one say quite loudly 'Vietnam!' at us, as if to ask where we were from so, I said 'England!' They jumped up, and I would be lying if I said that at first it wasn't a bit worrying, but they just wanted to shake hands with us. I was so glad we weren't American. Never have we been more proud to be English.

After that we thought a beer was on the cards and went into a café bar, where I pointed to a bottle of Heineken while Tony tried to order using his phrase book. Haha, my bottle came OK but Tony got an iced tea. Price of Heineken 30 pence, iced tea 10 pence, Tony's face priceless. It was even funnier trying to order garlic bread, and you know you can't help turning into Peter Kay - G-A-R-L-I-C- B-R-E-A-D.

13TH DECEMBER

After our evening of drinking tea and dodging army-clad Vietnamese we decided to head back to the hotel. where we checked out the bar area. It was the biggest bar I have ever seen in my life. There must have been two hundred chairs and tables.

We sat at a table overlooking the beach and tried to order a beer. They looked at us in total confusion, so we imitated drinking and thought they had got the message. We sat back and waited for our beer to arrive, but how sadly mistaken we were - they brought us coffee. After trying our best to refuse the coffee and re order the beer I took the waiter by the arm and led him across to the bar, where I went behind the counter and took two large bottles from the counter and smiled. He seemed to get the message and ran off returning with a huge bucket of ice.

They didn't seem to understand why anyone would want to drink cold beer, and looked totally confused when I then went back to the bar and took a few beers from the shelf and put them in the fridge. They giggled and laughed when they brought us the cold bottles. We hoped they would get the message and leave them in the fridge, but trying to tell them we would be back was very difficult.

'God Tony, look at this bloke' I said.' 'He's the image of Joseph Fritzell'

Tony immediately swung around, as I knew he would, and Joseph Fritzell then shouted 'do you mind if I come and join you?' (obviously, being European, we stood out.)

We smiled and said 'Yes' and he came over. 'Hello, my name is Manfred and I am from Austria.'

I nearly died, definitely Joseph's brother, or double.

After an hour I just watched his lips moving and laughed when he did and frowned when he did. He never shut up. I couldn't have followed him if I'd been on a bike. He was actually a nice bloke, so we didn't mind. I think because he was travelling alone and hadn't spoken to anyone for a while, he was enjoying the company. His wife and daughter didn't like travelling and had stayed at home! We didn't really say that much as we couldn't get a word in. I was more interested in persuading the staff to put more beer in the fridge.

Joseph kept on talking, so I decided to put more bottles in the fridge myself, getting a few strange looks from the staff. They laughed again and touched their foreheads, meaning, I presume, that we were mad.

14TH DECEMBER

At breakfast I was sketching away like Rolf Harris, but I still couldn't get any jam. I could draw a jar and write 'jam' on the side, but they can't read the words of course, so it is actually harder than you might think.

Joseph Fritzell joined us for breakfast and I could hardly remember what he had said last night. I was hoping he wasn't going to ask me anything. His lips were moving again and he was telling me that his wife was at home and his daughter did not like travelling. Now I could actually remember him telling me that because it made me more convinced he was Joseph Fritzell's brother.

He started to explain what the toots of the motor bikes meant. We had already figured it out, but he told us anyway. One toot meant 'I am behind yooo', two toots meant 'I vaunt to get past yooo' and three toots meant 'I am approaching you and I vaunt you tooo know I am coming past'. He then went on to tell us 'it is a lanvidge, a lanvidge'

We decided to move hostels, because the one across the road had got great reviews. We moved across the road to the Au Co Hotel, and who should we meet in reception but Joseph Fritzell again. We had assumed he was staying where we were originally, and now it looked as if we had moved to be with him. He was now acting like he was our new best friend. He was canny so we didn't mind too much, although he was shouting at the receptionist that his room had not been cleaned. 'It is not acceptable, not acceptable!' he shouted, his arms very animated.

We got the 'themed' room, which had four full-size ornamental trees in it. We had now been turned into Hansel and Gretel. Weird is not the word. The large oak-type tree was a wardrobe for Tony's vests and shorts. I was just hoping there were no birds in the tree, or worse still that Tony would not dream he was playing golf and decide to piss up it.

It was a stupid and rash decision, and I wished we had stayed at the Binh Duong Hotel, which was a million times nicer.

15TH DECEMBER

Lonely Planet said to check out X's cafe (for legal reasons I will only identify him as X) and sample the delicious cakes and buns on offer, so we went in search of it. I was so looking forward to tasting a nice bun, or anything really nice. X had come to Vietnam many years ago and loved it so much he moved there and opened a café and guesthouse.

Three hours and four domestics later we found it. There was the lovely X with green top and matching green teeth - they were 'summer teeth' (summer missing, summer black). The 'home baking' was displayed on the counter tops and resembled nothing you could possibly want to eat. The cakes were only a few dong and presumably the flies were free. To say I was gutted was an understatement.

We bought water, but decided against the cake. We quickly left and found a bar that sold alcohol. Our drinks were delivered to the table by a twelve-year-old waiter who put the two bottles of beer on the table, then returned with a huge bucket of ice - they just don't get the idea of serving cold beer. I know he was only twelve, but I could have hit him. I could have taken him out with one punch.

We walked around exploring and stumbled into the fresh meat and fish area. I have never seen so many women sitting in the street chopping meat and gutting fish with such professionalism. All the guts and waste was just discarded on to the street, literally a step away from the homes of people, single rooms with a bed and table and chairs along with a few personal bits and pieces dotted around. They were very friendly and waved and offered us their knifes to try some gutting, which I declined.

That afternoon we had a quick beer with Joseph Fritzell and managed to get the fridge well stocked up. The beer was ice cold now and Joseph also had them stock another fridge. We were sorted, or at least we thought we were. We found out when we got there that the 200 seats were now all occupied by wedding guests and worse than that, a few of them were trying the new brand of 'ice cold beer'. Shit! We managed to get some of them out of the fridge and hide them while we watched the rest being downed by drunken wedding guests.

This was our last night with Joseph, as we were travelling to Nha Trang the next day.

16TH DECEMBER - 27TH DECEMBER

We travelled on to Nha Trang, which is still in Vietnam but a more touristy area, and spent a little time at the local bus station, where I asked to use the toilet. The man gave me directions and off I went. I returned two minutes later as I couldn't find it, so he took me round the back and pushed open a door, which turned out to be the original door I had looked in.

The reason I hadn't thought it was the toilet was that there was nothing in it. It was just a shed with a concrete floor, no sink, no bin, no light, in fact no toilet. I said to him 'It's very nice of you to put a door and three walls around your paving slab' and he smiled at me as if he thought I was serious.

Our bus arrived, but instead of the large coach we thought we had booked a small minibus pulled up. The best seats were all taken, so they put us at the back, where there was no air con and the inside was stifling hot, like a microwave. It was a total nightmare. There was no room for our legs and we had to sit for six hours with our legs open to create space.

When we stopped at the rest stop I was like Heidi's friend who couldn't walk, and I thought I might need callipers. To make matters worse there was a huge spider on my leg. I was so delirious with the heat that I couldn't even be bothered to swipe it off.

We stopped for a toilet break, which was quite amusing because there weren't actually any toilets, but there was a very big field. After the bus station facilities I was not really surprised. We managed to get out of our seats without the help of a physiotherapist or callipers and staggered into the field. I was so hot that I didn't need the toilet, in fact I needed fluids, but I watched in amusement as everyone piled off the bus and ventured into the field.

Ten minutes later and we were all back on the bus to carry on with the journey from hell we had paid for. When we eventually arrived I can honestly say it was the first time I have ever had to keep my legs open for six hours.

Our hostel was the Hien Mai, a brand new hostel not long built, so it was immaculate. There are a lot of street robberies here at night, so we had to be a bit careful. Tony is only allowed the camera for short periods, so I keep it hidden most times.

In a pub we met four lads who all now live in Jersey, good crack. A jock lad, a scouser, a Brummie and a North East lad - it was like a scene from Auf Wiedersehen Pet.

Because of the pollution and the spitting, most of the people here wear masks (except the robbers, they're just blatant). The people here smoke so much they would have enough tar on their lungs to tarmac the M5 and half the A1. But the beach here is beautiful, and there are some great bars and restaurants.

They tell you to be careful with your drink, as 'spiking' is quite common, but somehow I don't think they would have much luck in getting anything into the top of our bottles as they were never out of our hands long enough. Besides, I don't think there would be much demand for naked photos of two pissed overweight Geordies, do you? However if you are interested or know anyone who is, I can sell you some photos.

The beer is cheap, good and cold, because they keep it in the fridge. Tony was drinking the shorts because they were so cheap - it's like a joke, 'so cheap they are guaranteed to make you blind'. He had the wrong glasses on and thought he'd gone blind. When he realised he wasn't he drank more.

CHRISTMAS EVE

Apart from occasionally being at work, I had never before been away from home for Christmas. We went on a boat trip with the Jersey lads. We had a great laugh, a free floating bar as long as you stayed in your floater! Tony hates going on a jet ski, so I jumped on with one of the lads. It was excellent and I even managed to throw him off the back at top speed, brilliant.

CHRISTMAS DAY

Had Christmas dinner at an American lads' bar called Booze & Cruise, with the Jersey lads, then spoke to the whole family on Skype at my brother James & Jackie's house. I took my laptop back to the hostel, as I didn't fancy getting robbed on Christmas night. I didn't fancy getting robbed any night.

BOXING DAY

One of the lads had paid for us all to go on another boat trip. We met up and sailed out into the ocean where the fun began. We went swimming and snorkelling and had another great laugh with great company.

27TH DECEMBER

We left Nha Trang in the afternoon and headed to Saigon (Ho Chi Minh City) on an overnight sleeper bus. We were sitting at the front of the bus, where we had the pleasure of the driver spitting out the window and talking on his phone the whole time. I was concerned that his spit was going to blow back in and land on me. Judging by his driving he was possibly the cousin of Stirling Moss. The positive side of things was that if we hit anything Tony and I were going to be in Saigon first.

For the last two hours of the journey from 4.30 am I watched the hustle and bustle of people setting up their stalls for work. Their life is hard and constant, no giros burning a hole in their shell suit bottoms here.

28TH DECEMBER

We arrived in Saigon to find it is manic. I have never seen so much traffic in my life. The population of Saigon appears to be many millions, and that's just in one street. I thought they must be all out on the streets today. It makes the London rush hour look like a day out on Holy Island.

We got off the bus at the main bus station and walked in the direction of where we needed to be. We were staying at the Thanh Thuong Hostel in District 1. After half an hour walking up and down the street we showed our map to a gentleman and were directed into a back lane. It was like a rabbit warren. There was a whole different area up and down the back lanes, an incredible place. There were houses and restaurants and the lanes were so narrow you could stand and touch the wall on both sides at once. I have never seen anything like it in my life. It was like a huge hidden city. Your neighbour's house was literally a paving slab away from yours. It was incredible, and I was genuinely speechless.

When we found the hostel the receptionist was fast asleep on the sofa, so I had to shake him awake and pull him up into a sitting position. I then pulled him to his feet while Tony held the bags! We were shown our room, which was very small but clean and tidy. Tony had to stand in the corner while I got ready, then I had to do the same or sit on the bed and wait.

That week there was a huge food festival taking place, with every culinary delight you could imagine. We watched a couple eating live snails, poking them with a stick to extract them from their shells and dipping them straight into vinegar. We declined the offer of a taste as my gag reflex was working overtime. There were some gorgeous stalls selling wonderful food, but I still wished there had been a Gregg's.

We sat with many other people and watched the water puppet show. I'm not sure what it was about, but it was lovely. There were lots of beautiful lights and dressed-up puppets.

We walked to the world-famous Ben Thanh Market, although I've never met anyone who has actually heard of it. It's extremely intense with tons of people coming up to you trying to sell you things. It's a nightmare - you can feel hands on you and people pulling you from all sides and the noise from everyone shouting together is unbearable. When we managed to get out it felt like we had escaped from a zoo.

Thankfully they had an area where they have 'set prices' and no bartering (for those who can't be bothered) and the prices were about £1.20 for a T-shirt. Some people enjoy bartering, me I can't be bothered. Just tell me the price and if I want it I will buy it.

29TH DECEMBER

Today we paid a very sombre visit to the war remnants museum. There were tanks, helicopters and military vehicles that had been left when the Americans left the country. Close up they were massive. There were three million Vietnamese killed in the war, including two million civilians, and three hundred thousand are still missing to this day. They're not likely to find them now.

Inside the museum it was very quiet. People were viewing items of memorabilia and the thousands of photographs, and a whole section displayed the horrors of 'agent orange'. People were visibly moved to tears as they looked at photo after photo of children with horrendous disfigurements. The American forces sprayed 72 million litres of herbicides (agent orange). Enormous bulldozers were used to rip up the jungle, agricultural land, villages, even cemeteries. In response the Vietcong used elephants because of their ability over rough terrain. These were bombed from the air along with other targets.

Chapter Six

CAMBODIA

30TH DECEMBER 2010

It was now time to head into Cambodia on the bus, which was pretty packed, so the smells were somewhat intense. I had so much tiger balm on my top lip it looked like I'd had Botox.

After a few hours we arrived at border control, where we all had to get off the bus with all our luggage and go through customs. We lined up, paid the 25 US dollars to get our visas and then headed off through customs. We then had to walk across the border for 'legal passage' and get back on to the bus (it was not allowed to cross the border with passengers). More women selling deep fried chicks and large hairy things (not sure what they were) were walking the length of the bus. Outside the window there were people everywhere arguing and buying and selling items. Everything imaginable was for sale, from vegetables to trinkets, from daggers to carpets. The aroma of food is very evident and my nostrils felt like they had been assaulted by the smell of decaying vegetation.

There were quite a few sellers on the bus as it waited to pull away, and they tried to sell us a DVD of Cambodian dance and music. I have quite an eclectic collection of music, but even I would be hard pushed to listen to Cambodian dance music. Believe me even Simon Cowell would say 'no thanks love'.

We boarded the bus again and crossed the border. Right across the line of the border are several big hotels, like a mini Las Vegas. If I had not seen it myself I would not have believed it. One was the Winn Casino and Hotel. It seems it is illegal to gamble in Vietnam, so they have built it as close to the border as possible on the Cambodian side.

After a few more hours of having to breathe through my nose and control my gag reflex we arrived in Phnom Penh, where three hundred people had been killed a week or so before when a bridge collapsed. You could feel the sadness in the air.

Phnom Penh is an amazing place with bustling activity. It is also littered with sad facts of life. There are between 10,000 and 20,000 children living on the streets. In Seim Reip and around the Ankor temples 1500 children live and work on the streets and nearly 1000 children live and work on the streets and beaches of Sihanoukville.

We managed to get off the bus in one piece after being pushed and shoved to the front. The tuk-tuk drivers were banging on the bus windows for business and we looked for one with an 'honest face'. They were all smiling and happy so it was hard to choose, but we opted for a little fella who reminded us of Kato from The Pink Panther. Good choice, reasonable fare, and his tuk-tuk might even have had an MoT. The noise was incredible, with horns blasting and people shouting and selling stuff, and it was stifling hot. There were people selling meat and fish from the pavement. To me it didn't look fit to eat, but some people were buying it. You could eat as much as you liked for two dollars. I think the results would have been quite obvious.

We had decided to stay at the Sweet Home hostel, but I wouldn't take the name of it to mean anything because it certainly wasn't sweet and it definitely was not home. However this was Cambodia. The staff were lovely and gave us a cold drink and showed us to our room. The bed was clean and we had an en suite shower room, which was all we needed.

We dumped our bags and went out into the main street, where the sellers were gathered in abundance. We tried a home-made local delicacy from a street seller, which tasted like hot sweet bread. It was quite nice, if a bit bland. The kids followed us and tried to sell us bangles and books.

We stopped at a roadside café to have a cold drink and watch what was going on. A little boy was sitting on the pavement watching us and we offered him a drink, so he sat with us and we bought him some chips. You would have thought we had given him a hundred pounds. The waiter told us he was one of hundreds of kids living on the streets. The boy said something to the waiter, who told us that he wanted us to see something, so we waited. After a few minutes he reappeared with his bicycle, and was obviously so proud of it. It looked as if it had spent most of its life in a canal waiting to be fished out, and it would have cost more in WD40 and wire wool to clean it up than it would have done to buy him a new one. I didn't think he'd be doing his cycling proficiency test on that.

31ST DECEMBER

The street outside our hostel was quite dusty and busy with tuk-tuk drivers trying for a fare. We took the best offer and hired a driver to take us to the infamous Killing Fields.

The journey took about twenty minutes. On the way we passed fields and little shacks on the side of the road. It was so hot and dry that the dust from the roads was getting in the back of our throats. There were people walking with huge bags and it was miles before any form of civilisation would appear, so its difficult to comprehend how long they must walk for.

At the entrance was a large memorial which displayed thousands of skulls of all different sizes ranging from adult to children. On the way in we lit a candle in remembrance of all the people who were massacred. Many thousands of people were slaughtered here and a lot of the mass graves remain untouched to this day. When it rains more bones and pieces of clothing are washed up, and these are kept and displayed on the site.

We saw teeth lying in the earth as we walked around. The walk around the fields was very moving and we found it hard to believe that this happened so recently. There were many mass graves.

A lone tree marked the spot where babies and children were killed by swinging them by their feet and smashing them against the tree, to save on bullets. There were many flowers laid at different places in remembrance of the dead. It is important to know that the Cambodian people encourage people to visit the site, as they want us to know the suffering that was caused, and more importantly that they have risen and are survivors. We were very quiet as we left the fields, trying to take it all in.

Next we visited S21, the torture chambers. This was originally a school, which makes it seem even more barbaric. Barely thirty years ago it was full of screams and death, and it's difficult to imagine that it was ever full of laughter and a safe place to be. We moved through the classrooms, which were all rigged up as various torture chambers, the metal beds and the electric wires that were used are still as they were, and the bricked-up corridors that were made into one-person cells still bear the scratchings on the walls.

There are hundreds of photographs on display of the people who perished here. Outside there are still the ropes that were used for hangings. You can't feel anything but sadness.

Next to the hanging area is a sign which reads:

1. You must answer according to my questions – don't turn them away.

2. Don't try to hide the facts by making pretexts this and that, you are strictly prohibited to contest me.

3. Don't be fool for you are a chap who dare to thwart the revolution.

4. You must immediately answer my questions without giving time to reflect.

5. Don't tell me about either your immoralities or the essence of the revolution.

6. While getting lashes or electrocution you must not cry at all.

7. Do nothing. Sit still and wait for my orders. If there is no order keep quiet when I ask you to do something you must do it right away without protesting.

8. Don't make pretext about Kampuchea Kron in order to hide your secret or traitor.

9. If you don't follow all the above rules you will receive many lashes of electric wire.

10. If you disobey any point of my regulations you shall get either ten lashes or five shocks of electric discharge.

During the Pol Pot régime, the adults of Cambodia would all have been fighting for survival on a daily basis. Many thousands of them perished. They are extremely poor people with the biggest hearts and hospitality. They are probably the most beautiful people I have ever had the privilege of meeting.

Phnom Penh has open sewers running through the streets and the smell is appalling around these areas. Even so, along the banks of the sewers there are people selling food and drinks, and people sit eating food and socialising. The smell is unbearable and I had to hold my hand over my face and nose. Yet the kids were playing in it.

We looked down and saw a dead dog floating on the top along with other indescribable items. The kids were poking the dog with a long stick. I don't even think our injections could have fought off any disease picked up from there. We couldn't make out whether the poor thing had fallen in and died or was thrown in after it had died. Once we moved away from here, the smell subsided and we saw the most beautiful temples and buildings.

NEW YEAR'S EVE

We celebrated the New Year at Rory's Bar, which is recommended in Lonely Planet. We had quite a good night and saw the New Year in with a few others. Some of the local 'ladyboys' called in, and one of them got a glass of wine and sat next to me with my pint! It was interesting to watch the lads becoming more 'familiar' as the night went on. It was strange singing Auld Lang Syne with a bunch of strangers though.

We had run up a tab behind the bar and were given our bill. They kept looking at us and seemed to be checking it over and over. Tony asked if there was a problem and they asked how many beers we had consumed. He told the truth, which was that he couldn't remember, but it was 'probably quite a few'. The beer was in small glasses and was reasonably cheap, so our bill was higher than they thought. It was no big deal though, and not enough to be looking at us with great interest. Tony joked that what we should have said was 'Yes we have drunk loads, but because your beer is so piss poor we are still standing'. I said 'we don't like to go under the two gallon bladder mark'. I think he might have believed us.

1ST JANUARY 2011

We watched the fishermen today on the river front, wading into the water up to their waists in the filthy brown water while the kids were swimming in it. It's anybody's guess as to what's in it.

2ND JANUARY 2011

This morning we boarded the local bus to Sihanoukville, Cambodia. We had bought two tickets for a seat each before we found out that some families had bought two tickets but had four and five of them on the two seats. And it was a five-hour journey!

We were sitting across from a family of four, two adults and two young kids, and an hour into the journey one of the kids started to be sick. You would think that the parents would have given him a bag but they didn't. They pushed his head forward so he could be sick all over the floor.

The smell was sickening, and I had tears in my eyes from the fumes off the vomit. We tried to avoid the splashes, but they kept on coming and I was turning green. No one else seemed to be bothered. The vomit was now two inches deep on the floor and swilling up and down the bus.

After a few looks from me they attempted to clean it up, using a plastic carrier bag. As you can probably imagine this made it even worse, as all they had done was spread it around the bus floor. There were lumps and bits of carrot everywhere and the smell was getting worse and worse. I was now practically delirious with the fumes.

Ten minutes later the bus pulled into a 'café'. I was so relieved that we could get off for some air, but the thought of eating was enough to make me want to be sick. The family of the sick child got off the bus without somehow skidding in the sick, although the mother did have vomit between her toes and her flip flops, and promptly got a seat and ordered their food! Within five minutes that bloody kid was gorging on sweets. I just knew that they would be regurgitated all over the floor.

After a short while we got back on the bus and the smell was even worse now as the thermometer was hitting 30 degrees. Half an hour later the kid turned a nice shade of green and the fucking sweets were up and all over the floor. Only another two hours to go.

We had yet another stop, this time for the toilet. Not everyone got off the bus, but the ones that did wandered off into the field. The men turned their backs and peed into the air and the women squatted. They peed and used their skirts as toilet roll, swiftly turning the wet bit to the back and getting back on the bus.

The smell now was a mixture of hot vomit and pissy skirts, in a temperature of about 35 degrees. While the bus stopped there were many sellers who barged on to it bus selling deep-fried chicks, locusts, cockroaches and other indescribable foods. A few of them had bought the deep-fried chicks and were tucking into them. One woman sitting near us was sucking on what looked like something from a bush tucker trail! We were not really hungry.

After driving through nothingness for ages we arrived at Sihanoukville, where our first impressions were total shock. There was rubbish and bin bags everywhere and smashed building bricks all over the place. It was difficult to tell if it was building work or demolition going on. There was a little girl playing in the rubble of something that had definitely been demolished.

Despite the state of the place it was very friendly and a nice safe place to be. We wandered the street and found our hostel, checked in and got issued with a free mosquito net, so we were happy with that. The room was very basic to say the least. It only had two single beds and a toilet and shower. The white sheets were crisp and clean though.

We got directions and had a wander to the beach which was a five-minute stroll away. There were plenty of places en route to eat and drink. It is incredibly cheap in Sihanoukville.

The beach was packed and had a great atmosphere, and we found loads of bars and eating places, too many to choose from. We watched the manager of a restaurant trying to entice people in, but we had just watched him covering one nostril and blow his snot out of the other one, so we gave that one a miss.

3RD JANUARY

On recommendation from our hostel we caught a local tuk-tuk to take us to a beach called Otres. This is a stunning beach, crystal clear blue water and no sellers. On Otres there is one private hotel that has its own stretch of sand and sun beds. Further along it is very quiet, with a few little beach bars that have free beds if you stay and use their facilities. The food is really good along the shoreline so it's nice to spend the whole day here.

We bumped into the Jersey Boys, who had also travelled into Cambodia from Vietnam, so we had a few beers with them and watched the sun go down. There are a lot of street kids working on the beach who collect the empty cans. For every 100 cans they collect they earn one dollar. We donated quite a few cans to their bin liners. By the time we left they could have afforded to take their families out for a meal to Gordon Ramsey's restaurant. In all seriousness your heart bleeds when you see their plight.

4TH JANUARY

We checked out the beaches today and had a good look about the place. I was asked today about 200 times if I wanted a massage. I would rather poke cocktail sticks in my eyes, I hate being faffed over. I also refused to buy a bracelet from a seller so she has cursed me to break one of my fingers. So apart from that there isn't really any of the 'hard sell'!

We sat in a beach bar and watched the kids selling their little trinkets up and down the beach. Tourists are discouraged from buying from the children as it encourages them to continue selling, and more importantly it stops them from going to school. All the children get free education but they can make money on the beach. It's very sad, because a lot of these children are the main earners for their family. If they don't sell they earn no money, a vicious circle for them. No school, no education, no selling, no money. I don't know what the answer is.

5TH JANUARY

We had quite a few beers tonight and ventured into a lovely rooftop restaurant. It was all lit up with sparkling lights and music playing. Once we had climbed the stairs we were immediately in the 'restaurant', where there were chairs and tables placed around the room. We sat down and quickly a waiter appeared at our table. He took our order of two large beers and promptly returned with them. We were the only people in, and we sat looking over the balcony into the main street below, watching the people coming and going and how the taxi drivers operated.

I saw a cat sitting at Tony's feet and reached down to stroke it. It moved pretty quickly, and so did we when we realised it was a rat. It was bloody massive. It ran down the stairs into the street where it looked around and promptly came back up the stairs back into the restaurant (I use the word 'restaurant' very loosely). We quickly drank our beers and left. The next morning when we saw the place we could not believe it. It is amazing how a few fairy lights and a lot of alcohol can make things look great.

7TH JANUARY

On the beach the touts go up and down giving flyers out. A young lad tried to get past us and I asked why he hadn't given me a flyer. I enjoyed watching him squirm as he tried to explain it was for the new night club opening.

'Do you think I'm too old to come?' I said.

'No no, I didn't see you' he said.

'Well I'll have a flyer then please'

'Yes, that's OK. Do you think your dad will want one?' and he pointed to Tony, who was oblivious to this and singing along to Doris Day on his MP3 player.

There was a 'cinema' facing our hostel (well, it was advertised as a cinema). All the latest movies were neatly displayed on posters. The staff were all female and aged from eighteen to twenty. Their 'uniform' was a small skirt and top with high shoes/boots. The customers were all male and in the same age group. All the 'movies' lasted half an hour! We seemed to be the only people who had noticed this. We sat and watched the taxis arriving with young lads and taking them away half an hour later.

We decided to move hostels, as the walls in our room didn't go right to the ceiling and you could hear everything. In fact if you had stood on a chair you would have been able to see over the top. It had dusty wooden floor boards and was very basic. The couple upstairs must have been on honeymoon as it was like Geppetto's work shop in our room.

We had the privilege of listening to three lads who were rating their prostitutes for looks and price. One lad in particular was quite upset at the service he had received and wouldn't be using her again. He had probably only gone to see Return of the Jedi.

We moved across the road to the Beach Road Hotel, which was dead cheap and had a gorgeous swimming pool, which was brilliant, especially as the beach got so packed, even more so at the weekends when the locals descended in their droves. I suppose it was their beach.

Within a week the whole place was looking better as the clean-up began. Although people were cleaning up nothing appeared to have any order to it. Men were laying pavements on top of rubble that had not been flattened. Even I knew it should have had a whacker plate over the top of it. There was a wall about twenty metres long and half a metre high being painted white at one end while it was being demolished at the other end. I cannot think to this day what the logic was.

After a few days some heavy machinery started to arrive, a digger, a tractor, and a dumper truck. The digger and the dumper truck I could probably imagine being put to use, but the tractor was, and still is, a mystery. The health and safety wear was all in the shape of shorts, vests and the obligatory flip-flops. A couple of them had finished off the look with sunglasses.

Near to our hostel was a 'natural thinking hospital' where they claimed you could think yourself back to health. It's an interesting thought and you can be a cynic, but personally I don't think you can beat a bit of anaesthetic and morphine. Chant as much as you like but I'm away to casualty.

14 JANUARY

We had to endure another four-hour bus journey back to Phnom Penh. It was a luxury bus with curtains and free sick bags (when the floor's full use the bag). We got the seats right behind the driver, who had obviously been separated at birth from Jackie Stewart. Our knuckles were white.

At one point a large truck was coming towards us and I was thinking, 'He's never gonna make it, he's never gonna make it...' and the truck was getting nearer and nearer towards us. Then at the last minute, our driver did a last-minute swerve, blasted his horn and started cursing and swearing. I thought, here it's a case of who's got the biggest balls. We were on a death wish, and at this point I wasn't sure we were ever going to reach our destination.

The bus was full of mosquitoes and I must have killed twenty in a few minutes by clapping my hands on them. I saw one flying around me and successfully clapped my hands on it, killing it dead, but the bus driver nearly shat himself and we almost careered off the road. I then had to blow on them for the duration of the journey as they flew around my face. When I got off the bus at the toilet stop (another field) the driver smiled a smile of brown teeth and winked at me. I think he thought I had been blowing in his hair deliberately. For the rest of the journey my face was wrapped in my T-shirt.

Further down the road we passed a bus crash and saw lots of people on the side of the road, though no one seemed bothered about it except us. A few hours later we arrived back at Phnom Penh, where we returned to the same hostel as before. Yes it was basic, but it was central and the beds were clean. By this point I was unfortunately vomiting like Linda Blair, so went straight to the room. On the way upstairs I was offered a bowl of 'khmer' curry that looked and smelt like the dead dog that was floating in the sewer. God only knows what it would have grown if you had put some in a petri dish. I said a polite 'no thanks' and rushed to my room. The room we had got this time was on the top floor and had bars on the windows and a walk-out balcony with an old settee on that was covered in some type of leather. Unfortunately I never got to sit out there as I was feeling shit.

15TH JANUARY

Thankfully I was feeling better this morning as we had to catch the bus to Sein Reip, a six hour journey. I hadn't eaten properly now for a few days and was feeling like Bobby Sands. The bus was packed as usual. We had a screaming baby behind us who definitely would have won the title for shitting its nappy as many times as it could in one hour. I was wondering about the baby's diet and if it was fed on khmer curry. If the smell wasn't bad enough someone got their packed lunch out and my 'barfometer' was now on overdrive. It smelt like something had died in a Tupperware box. It should have been sent to the crematorium. For the six hours I had to hold a paper tissue over my nose soaked in tiger balm. I was practically delirious with the aroma of the balm.

Thankfully it wasn't long before we were pulling into the bus station. When the bus stopped the usual banging on the windows and shouting from the waiting tuk-tuk drivers began. We had a free pick-up from our hostel, so we didn't have to go through the rigmarole of choosing a driver. Our driver approached us with a placard with our name on. 'Mr Hansell, Mr Hansell!' he was shouting, like little Tattoo from fantasy island. He took us to the Garden Inn hostel, which had only been built a year previous and was gorgeous inside. It had a fabulous dark wooden staircase like the one in Gone With The Wind.

We went on to 'Pub Street' and watched the Mackems 1 – Newcastle 1 match. Pub Street is lined with pubs and restaurants and closed off in the early evenings to sellers and beggars, which means that when you have suffered 'beggar's fatigue' during the day you can sit and relax while you eat and drink.

17TH JAN - 20TH JAN

We had a free breakfast the next morning, which was very nice. We had a driver for the day to take us to the temples. We made sure we had everything we needed for our day out - the camera and the money. Tony was talking, so I decided to slope off discreetly and wait for him in the tuk-tuk. I stepped into it, and as I went to sit down it toppled over. I was lying underneath it shouting 'I'm OK, I'm OK!' and trying my best to keep myself composed while the little six-stone Cambodian driver was attempting to get it off me. I think he was more concerned about his tuk-tuk than me. Tony gave him a hand, and between them they got me up. There was nothing damaged except my pride, the wing mirror, the front bumper and the petrol tank.

When I had dusted myself down and had been helped back into it (breathing in, as if that was going to help!) by him holding on to it for dear life, we headed off to see the temples. We drove out through the villages and on to the main roads, where we watched the sellers on the sides of the roads and listened to the constant tooting of moped and tuk-tuk horns. The noise was non-stop.

About fifteen minutes into the journey our driver was signalled and stopped by another driver. He told us the police were checking documents at the temple and as he didn't have a licence he would have to drive around until the police had left. This is quite incredible, but a daily occurrence. I was now hoping that the police were not going to be out all day, because I was looking forward to seeing the temples. I tried to imagine how poor he must be because the fakes you can purchase in Vietnam for a very small price are pretty convincing. I felt like buying him a driving licence on the black market, but the thought of doing time in the Cambodian Hilton for assisting an offender scared the shit out of me.

He took us off on a mystery tour, driving around and around, and I was convinced we were going in circles. The oak tree was on the left, then it was on the right, then on the left again, until we realised that yes we were going round in circles. It was laughable, but we didn't mind because it was red hot and we did feel sorry for him.

We stopped to feed some wild monkeys in a lovely quiet tree-lined area, but when we got out we were practically mugged by kids selling bananas. They must have been hiding behind the trees to swoop on us when they could. I wouldn't mind, but the monkeys didn't even want the bananas.

When we got back into the tuk-tuk our driver produced a photograph from his pocket and showed it to us. He asked in broken English if we thought it looked like him. The photo of whoever it was looked like it been taken over forty years ago. It definitely wasn't him. We shook our heads and laughed and he put it back in his pocket.

We now had to drive around again. After about an hour, the coast was clear and we arrived at Angkor Wat, which was the most beautiful sight. He told us to spend as long as we wanted - he would wait for us. The temple was amazing and the sheer size of it was incredible. The colour of the stonework was a drab grey but against the blue sky it was beautiful.

After a while we returned to find him waiting for us. We then went to Angkor Thom, which was still beautiful but pretty much ruined by the Khmer Rouge. The faces in the stones were incredible, but as at Angkor Wat the plans had been destroyed during the Pol Pot regime by the Khmer Rouge.

The process of rebuilding will take years. If you can imagine a huge mansion being demolished, then having to put it back together brick by brick without any plans, that's just a small-scale version of what they have to do. Hopefully with the intervention of some fantastic historians and architects they will one day manage to get it put back to the way it might have looked originally.

Finally we went to the temple where the film Tomb Raider was shot. It was lovely. All the trees had grown into the brickwork and it looked amazing. The stone was grey and black and if you were lucky enough to catch sight of a monk in orange robes the contrast was beautiful.

On the way back we stopped off at our driver's 'friend's' jewellery shop. He asked us to just look, as every visitor he took got a voucher, and the vouchers could be exchanged for petrol. I felt like saying 'Just drive to the garage and I'll put a few quid in for you, I can't be doing with looking at any more bloody jewellery'. I wouldn't mind, but it's jewellery like Elizabeth Taylor wore in Cleopatra.

Visited Pub Street that night and the beer was only 50p a pint, plus I found the most fantastic little place that sold tapas and nachos. The pubs and restaurants were busy and we had a beer in the rooftop restaurant Angelina Jolie frequented while filming. As you'd expect they had photographs up and were selling a 'Tomb Raider' cocktail.

We watched the 'working girls' touting for business and getting a fair number of customers. That was until the ladyboys arrived, parading up and down with their high heels and fantastic legs and stealing their trade. It was incredible to watch. Tony and I played the game, trying to guess who was male or female, but after a few beers it was hard to tell. The local drunk eventually stole the show swatting imaginary flies from his face and chasing imaginary dogs. God only knows what he had been drinking, but he was definitely hallucinating.

We headed back to the hostel and got followed by a tuk-tuk driver wanting to take us for the fare. We tried explaining that we were staying only five minutes away but he wouldn't have it. He followed us for so long that we were practically outside the hostel door.

20TH JANUARY

In the morning we caught the 7 am bus back to Bangkok. We were hemmed in like sardines in a tin, with the luggage piled high in the aisle. It was impossible to see anyone else on the other seats for rucksacks. If we needed to be out you had no chance. We had good views from the window though, and when we passed a school we could see the kids working in the fields with their little sandals on and swinging machetes, no long winded 'risk assessment' here. I bet the teachers are allowed to apply a bit of Savlon without a note from the parents or the Prime Minister.

Learning the necessary skills of gardening is probably one of the most important lessons here, as it is inevitably going to be a future for most of them. We passed fields and saw the workers up to their knees working on their rice crops. It looked like back-breaking work as the heat was in the thirties.

Soon we arrived at the Thailand checkpoint, where we had to wait until all the luggage had been taken off the bus. We then had to queue with our passports to be checked into the country. What a nightmare that was. We lined up and were all given a sticker to wear for our onward journey. Once you were wearing the sticker you were allowed back on the bus for all of five minutes before we had to get back off and cross the border on foot. I stood with one foot in Cambodia and one foot in Thailand.

One of the scams was a couple of official-looking men who took your luggage from you, loaded it on to a trolley and pushed it across the border, where they told you you could claim your luggage. At this point they tried to charge you several US dollars. In fact they were just chancers. You can carry your own luggage and tell them to sod off, which is what we did.

Once across the border we were ushered to a waiting area which was in the sun and roasting hot, as there were no seats or shade. There were quite a few beggars milling around and my heart was broken watching a girl of about seven years old with a small baby of about six months on her hip. They were both in filthy rags and the baby's bottom, face and hands were covered in sores and scabs. The little girl was begging for a drink of water. Her lips were cracked and looking at her it was plain to see she was dehydrated.

It was hard to watch people turning their backs and carrying on drinking their water. I was choking and red hot but I gave her my water. The little girl didn't drink any of it herself but sat and poured it into the baby's mouth. It was the saddest thing I have ever seen in my life. We were then moved into another area where the little girl wasn't allowed, and we never saw her again.

We queued for two hours until we were allowed through. People were moaning that they had to wait, and I couldn't stop thinking of the little girl and baby I had just witnessed and how selfish people can be. There was a girl about nineteen years old with a terribly swollen face and one eye closed, and we could hear her telling others that she had been travelling back into Thailand for medical care because she had been bitten by bedbugs. This was one of the people who had stood and drank their water in front of the little girl with the baby, so my sympathy was lost on her.

We eventually got through and on to our designated bus. Tony's sticker had fallen off his T-shirt and when he tried to convince the driver that he was with me I played with the idea of pretending I didn't know him, but decided against it when I saw the size of his gun. After a few minutes they allowed him on, and we thought we were about to drive away when a menacing looking official got on the bus with a huge gun thrown over his chest. He started pointing it at a couple of Thais and we were terrified to look. When he was quite satisfied they were not smuggling anyone into the country off he went. We all gave a sigh of relief and the Cambodians we had smuggled on to the bus came out of the luggage racks (No, I made the last bit up.)

We arrived back at the Sanawan and after showing the driver of the bus the card he dropped us a ten-minute walk away on a busy motorway. The people on the bus must have been wondering where we were going. We walked until we came across a real traditional Thai village, whose inhabitants were quite shocked at seeing two tourists passing through with rucksacks. But they were more than friendly, and a few of them even invited us into their homes to stay.

We had stayed at the Sanawan Hotel before because it's so near the airport, and we had a flight again from there so we returned. We checked in and got a lovely room along from the pool. While I was sitting reading the menu the owner heard me say that I was fed up of noodles and rice, and he said to me 'Would you like me to make you some egg and chips?' It was a true Shirley Valentine moment. It turned out that he was from originally from Whitby and his name was Dick. And to top it all his egg and chips were bloody lovely. Mind you he did tell me to fry my own egg, which I did.

21ST JANUARY

We were in the area of Bangplee, where the population was very small. It's not actually on the tourist route either, so it's very traditional. The locals here are very friendly and helpful, I wish I could say the same thing about their guard dogs. They waved and posed for photos and attempted to teach us Thai and in return we taught them a few words of English. Many Thais must now be walking around Bangplee shouting 'TOON TOON, TOON ARMY!'.

We needed to cross the river to the market and were told by Dick from our hostel to use the boat bridge. We didn't think anything of it until we got to the river and realised that the boat bridge was actually two rowing boats tied together which you walk across, then pay a penny at the other end. There was talk of a bridge being built across the river, but the locals objected and instead came up with the idea of the boats. It's very Heath Robinson, but it works and it hasn't spoilt the river or the landscape.

There is definitely a knack in walking in small rowing boats, one I haven't quite mastered it yet. The locals walk across without effort and the boat doesn't even move. We walk across and it's like walking in custard, we are all over the place, much to the delight of the village people (not the ones who sing YMCA) who have now congregated on the river bank.

As we reach the other side we are met with great applause and laughs. The fortune tellers and sellers of food and vegetables line the banks and we collect our supplies. 'Oh I see you on boats, you velly shaky' one gentleman said. We cracked on a bit with the people we met while shopping and soon it was time to attempt the boat walk again. Personally I would have been a black coat and opted for a proper bridge, but then they would have probably ostracised me from the village anyway.

I stepped on to the boat and with all my effort still couldn't keep the thing from moving. There were laughs and claps as I walked the walk of shame and paid my penny. Then I curtsied to them and they clapped as we wandered off.

Chapter Seven

MALAYSIA

22ND JANUARY 2011

Time to fly on to Malaysia. We left the hotel and headed to the airport in a local taxi, which cost about a quid in our money. A bit more expensive than the local bus, but so cheap it wasn't worth the hassle. As usual we waited around the airport and eventually boarded our flight to Penang.

On arriving we collected our luggage and jumped into a taxi outside the terminal to get to our accommodation. En route we passed through a very affluent area where the taxi driver told us the 'rich and famous' lived. I asked who, and he pointed out the famous shoe man Jimmy Choo's house. I don't know if me and Jimmy would get on as I refuse to wear anything else but Doc Martens. Apparently Mr Choo sometimes still works in the shop in Penang, so if you were really lucky you could be served by him. I would still tell him I prefer DMs.

We were staying with a Muslim family at a home stay called Baan Talay. We pulled up at the gate and it was a house in the art deco style, metal window frames and lots of garden - it looked lovely. We made our way inside and were met by the owner and his wife, who were very nice. They showed us to the room where we would be staying. It had been built on the side of their garage using plywood and sticky-back plastic. He threw the door open as if to say 'dah dah!' and we were faced with a sign on the wall that said 'NO ALCOHOL'.

The Betty Ford clinic flashed through my mind and I knew it was going to be a long night.

The room itself was actually OK and the bed was nice and clean. We got settled in and set off for a walk around to see what was on offer in the area. We were a two-minute walk from the beach, which was, or could have been beautiful, but unfortunately it was littered with tyres and rubbish that people had dumped. It was a great shame, because the area was small and the beach very secluded. We walked along anyway and took in the local sights. We were the only two people on the beach, which stretched for miles.

After a while we started to get a bit peckish and found a place called the Hawkers Centre, which was basically a huge corrugated roof with hundreds of plastic tables and chairs underneath. Local traditional cooks would then turn up with their stainless-steel carts, woks, ovens and cooking utensils and turn out the most amazing food for literally coppers. You can choose from vegetarian to seafood, where you get to choose what you want from the tanks on show, and there are loads of meat stalls.

We ate and watched the locals ordering. If it looked good we tried to remember what it was called so we could have it another night.

23RD JANUARY

Just as I was getting off to sleep I spotted a huge lizard on the wall, I would have left it, but it kept on making a hissing noise, so I had to get up and get it out the room. After what seemed like forever it finally made its exit, hopefully never to return.

After a good night's sleep we woke early and decided to get up to sample the free breakfast. The kitchen was lovely and there were a few others also staying. The owner had a hired help who was doing the breakfasts. The owner chatted to us over breakfast and told us he had forgotten to take down the 'no alcohol' sign, from our room, and we could feel free about drinking. After sensing that the other guests were also relieved, we had a laugh about it. So straight after breakfast we got a taxi to the off licence (no, not really).

After we had finished eating we caught the local bus along to the beach. The beach was gorgeous, very unspoilt and uninhabited except for a couple of little cafés selling the usual cold drinks and snacks. We found a lovely spot on the sand and watched the waves. There were a few stray dogs on the beach, and we had to be careful as a month before on the same beach a young German tourist had been killed by three savage dogs.

After an hour the weather suddenly changed and we noticed the cafés were collecting their chairs and umbrellas and putting them away. We had no sooner decided to move than the sky went black and the wind whipped up a storm. The rain started pouring down and thunder and lightning was shooting across the sky. The noise was as loud as a jet plane, it was incredible, and we had to shout to hear each other.

It was amusing watching a couple of the local lads trying to get a couple of people back in on jet skis. Some came in quicker than the lightning, but others thought it was great, so they took ages. We got under cover at the beach bar but we weren't convinced the whole lot wouldn't blow away.

The storm lasted about two hours and it was incredible. The noise, the colours from the lightning and the sea lashing against the sand were spectacular. Once the rain had stopped we made a run for it and caught the bus back along to the house. Some people were completely soaked on the bus and others had evidently been on it when the storm started and were bone dry.

The bus dropped us off at the top of the road where we were staying and we went into the Hawkers for some food, meeting up with a few other people who were also staying at the Baan Talay. We sat with them, they were younger than us, nice people. I opted for the vegetarian dish - I couldn't begin to imagine why anyone would want to eat some of the stuff on offer. I sat and watched a lady eating a thing that resembled a bed bug magnified a million times. It filled her whole plate, and she was breaking the shell and scooping out this meat that looked like green vomit.

After dinner we walked back to the hostel and found a little kitten locked in our bedroom. It must have sneaked in when our room was cleaned. He was gorgeous and I wanted to keep him.

24TH JANUARY

After breakfast the next morning we caught the local bus to Georgetown. This was a big place with loads of shops, hostels, cafés and restaurants. It was very commercialised compared to where we were staying. We walked around and saw the various temples and churches. We had now seen more temples and churches than you could shake a stick at. We were so pleased that we had opted to stay with a traditional Muslim family on the outskirts.

25TH JANUARY

We got a lift from the owner to a really secluded beach. There was only Tony and me and some paragliders in the distance, so this was what you could call secluded.

We were sitting on the beach watching the world go by and admiring one of the gliders flying along weightless, like a bird, when suddenly he fell. We were shocked, but he was so far away there was nothing we could do to help. He must have fallen about ten feet on to the sand and had to be hurt, though we could see he was moving.

A few people rushed over to him and he was helped up and moved to a seat.

They promptly packed away the one that had snapped and the flying soon resumed with new customers. The beach must have been five football pitches long and they were getting closer and closer to where we were sat. Ten minutes later I looked up and saw a paraglider coming right for us. We jumped up and tried to move but he landed right on top of us. We were buried in his silk parachute as people came running to help us out. They managed to free us from the tangled mess and were very apologetic. They offered us a free ride, which we quickly declined.

The sky went black and we knew another storm was coming. If I had known a storm was coming five minutes earlier I could have made a tent from the parachute. Again everyone ran for cover, two days in a row, the café owner must have been rubbing his hands. Eventually the storm subsided and we jumped on the bus back to the house.

At tea time we went to another Hawkers place and watched a woman eating something that resembled the sort of thing you weigh at a post mortem. We had absolutely no idea what it was. I wasn't very hungry.

There was another big storm the next day.

27TH JANUARY

As we had been going along the coast by bus to the beach we had passed a sign advertising 'Penang's largest toy museum, complete with interactive toys and games'. I couldn't wait. Tony didn't want to go and said it couldn't be that big because the building it was in was absolutely tiny. In fact there was another big building behind it and I assumed the museum was housed in that. Tony said it would be shit, but I was convinced it must be in the adjoining building, so off we went on the bus and arrived and paid our money.

In the entrance as we went in was a big tired-looking teddy bear that said 'argggg'! That was the interactive bit. Tony's face was saying he'd been right, but I wanted to give it a chance. Once inside it was easy to establish that this had been a collector who had run out of space for his hobby. There were glass cabinets full of everything from Action Men to Star Wars characters, to name but a few. It would be the largest toy museum in Penang – it was the only toy museum in Penang. I hated admitting it to Tony, but he was right, it was shit. And now he had a smug look on his face.

29TH JANUARY

After breakfast the owner kindly gave us a lift to the ferry terminal. We got our tickets and boarded the ferry to Langkawi. I was one of the few women not dressed in a burka. We got on board and it was surprisingly nice, apart from a huge cockroach which ran behind the speaker on the wall.

Cockroaches are just horrible. There was a Muslim woman in a full burka who went outside on deck with her friend, who was wearing the same. They were taking photos from the boat and I was sitting watching them. They were totally oblivious to the fact that there was a blacked out window, so we could see out but they couldn't see in. One of them removed her face cover for her friend to take her picture and her smile displayed a set of teeth and gums no self-respecting dentist has ever seen. Without being accused of being racist, if she was my wife I would make her wear that face cover as well. If this was an arranged marriage then someone must hate their son, because you would never inflict someone that ugly on someone you loved. You can imagine her going into Boots for her photos and the assistant saying 'Have you seen this ugly bastard, let's hope she never takes that off her face again, that's six ninety nine please'.

As we were coming in to land I saw a Mecca sign and thought, great, they have bingo. There were crowds of people waiting to board the next ferry, and people waiting to meet friends and relatives from ours. Not too many tourists stay here, so we decided to give it a go for a couple of nights. We got a room at the Eagle Bay Hotel on the fifteenth floor, so the views were great, we could see the tops of the mosques all painted gold and glinting in the sunlight.

The hotel has a small swimming pool which we could see from our window. It was a strange affair, built on top of what looked like a garage. You went up a ladder and got straight into the pool. The water touched the sides, so there was only one way in and one way out and no walkway round the pool. There was a lady fully clothed in full burka swimming up and down the pool. I wondered if she was doing her swimming badge. We did ours in pyjamas.

30TH JANUARY

We came down for breakfast after being up from 4 am with the mosque directly in front of our window. There were so many shoes outside it looked like a branch of Freeman Hardy Willis. The breakfast menu was curry, noodles, rice and a few other unidentifiable dishes, but I found some bread and butter so we could have a real feast. Several pieces of toast later we'd had several strange looks as we refused to get stuck into the curry. I couldn't even think of eating curry and rice for breakfast, never mind using my fingers to eat it with.

After we had eaten our toast we returned to our room, then two minutes later we were going into town. We had to walk quite a way, but the walk was nice. We passed a school and watched the schoolchildren playing. All the little girls were dressed in pale blue dresses and matching head scarves, and the little boys had pale blue shirts on.

I hadn't been outside for long when I was stung by a long black flying thing. I'm not sure what it was, but my arm was bleeding from the bite and I was waiting to die. Tony told me to give it a couple of hours to see what happened. Not sure if he meant that in a sympathetic way or not. We went out exploring the area, and I wasn't sure if the delirium was from the smells and the heat or the sting on my arm. Tony told me to pull myself together and stop going on about it. He said I was attention seeking. I was now hoping I was seriously ill just to prove him wrong.

31ST JANUARY

I discovered I wasn't dead at 4 am when the mosque started its morning disco. At breakfast we were asked for our ticket - apparently you need a ticket for the breakfast in case you are sneaking in to get it for free. Yesterday we tried sneaking out and got caught because we had 'not eaten much'. I somehow didn't think there was a big demand for tickets for this breakfast on the black market. I can't believe that we had to convince the lady we were booked in here. The receptionist came over and assured her we were guests of the hotel.

We said thank you to her, and then thought it would have been easier not to have come in for breakfast after we had seen the selection. I can't believe I was actually looking forward to bread and butter. If we had been international drug smugglers we would have got more than bread and butter for breakfast. Although maybe not in this country.

We stuffed our faces with the bread and butter and decided, as we had been up since 4 am, to have a lie down. I played with the idea of moving the 'qiblat' (the sign pointing to Mecca) from the ceiling and putting it in the other corner, but I'm not sure if Allah would have got the joke. I've never met the man so I don't know his sense of humour.

If I thought he could take a joke I would sneak into the mosque at five to four and shout 'Oggie, oggie, oggie!' Or hide all their flip-flops for when they came out.

After a nap we walked into town, where we browsed through a few of the local shops. There were a few tramps lying on park benches with their clothing and belongings in bags. We saw a hostel place that had security gates on the inside of the doorway. It was like the Salvation Army Hostels we have in the UK.

I kid you not, the hostel was called the Sunderland Motel.

1ST FEBRUARY

When we had arrived at the Eagle Bay we'd had to put our valuables in the safe, so now we had to retrieve them, as we were leaving to travel to another area. The process was pretty much the same as when we arrived. It was comical, we were shown into a proper vault by a gun-wearing security man and the box was opened for us. We were then left to place our valuables in a metre-long security drawer. We held one key and the hotel held the other. It was like a Michael Caine movie. Behind the screen we opened the vault, stifling our giggling, and deposited our valuables, which consisted of two passports and a Nokia mobile with the 'A' button missing. They didn't know that though. We came out of the vault like Elizabeth Taylor and Richard Burton. Bet Richard Burton never had a Nokia phone with the A button missing. The receptionist called us a taxi to take us to Pantai Chenang, on the beach.

The driver spoke no English, and sang some Muslim song all the way there. We walked around and eventually booked a room at the Best Motel in a wooden bungalow. The bungalow was lovely, all polished wood, but it was quite expensive because it was Chinese New Year.

We dumped our bags and went straight off to check out the beach and have a swim. We found one part of the beach was beautiful and the other, which was quite populated, was not so nice, loads of fag ends and crap on the sand. There were plenty of places to eat and drink and most of the beer was about 80p a pint and buy one get one free. This was good news, and the alcohol would surely make the beach look nicer. We were not too impressed, so we decided to gate crash a four-star hotel called the Aseania. They could only ask us to leave, so we went for it.

We walked in and got a sun bed – marvellous. We spent the whole day there and decided to come back tomorrow as it was better than the beach. The pool here was once the largest in Asia. It was divided into different sections - one pool was actually a river, there was a pool that resembled walking into the sea with a rough surface, which got deeper as you waded in, then three pools which were all cleverly joined in places with slides and waterfalls. You could see how beautiful it had been in its heyday, but now it was desperately in need of a facelift.

I spent all day pushing in front of the kids to go on the slides. Let them wait, adults first, kids never learn anything if you let them have everything their way. After a while of going up and down the slide I got tired of it and the water kept going up my nose.

There was a lovely pool bar, which was great because you could sit there and drink as much as you want and pee at the same time. I think we might get Paul, our club steward, to open one in the club car park.

After a while we headed back along the main street in the direction of our hostel and called in for a few beers just to sample the ones on offer. After several, we decided they were all good and we should sample more later on.

We got changed and watched the sunset on the beach. It was much cooler now, so the locals now descended on to the beach and participated in the water sports on offer. We watched the banana go out with five women dressed in full burka. I admired them - I once came off wearing a bikini and it was hard enough getting back on anyway, never mind with all that heavy wet fabric. Their men were waiting for them in Speedos.

2ND FEBRUARY

I bought myself some new flip flops today, which were quite 'girlie' for my standards in a nice shade of lilac, but mainly I bought them because they were cheap. I also bought an industrial-size tin of mosquito and insect spray, after being bitten by either one huge mosquito or several. I sprayed the room and went out, and when I came back I found two massive dead cockroaches in the bathroom, so it definitely worked. So much for the gorgeous bungalow, I was now terrified to go to the toilet through the night.

We gate-crashed the Aseania hotel again today, and they welcomed us in - they obviously thought we were staying there. If they asked we would have owned up, but they didn't, so no crime in that surely.

My sister Sharron, AKA Hyacinth Bouquet, and her husband Vince were arriving the next day for two weeks' holiday with us, so Tony and I were excited.

Because of the Chinese New Year the place was very busy with restaurants all offering the 'best meal in Langkawi'. They had their tanks out on the pavement and the fish were swimming on death row, desperately breathing in and trying to look thin so as not be picked. The fat ones had no chance. Some were probably just going to give themselves up and get it over with. We saw a lady looking in the tank and I could swear one of the fish was trying to hide behind another. I had to walk away as he scooped the fish out, knowing it was going to be murdered.

4TH FEBRUARY

Tony told me he was pleased I had slept well as when he'd got up through the night to go to the bathroom there were cockroaches in abundance. Thankfully in the afternoon we moved to the Palms guest house, a very nice hostel. We waited at the hostel for Hyacinth and Vince to arrive, and every time a taxi pulled in we were jumping up to see if it was them.

After what seemed like ages they eventually arrived. I ran to greet them with my arms outstretched to give them a cuddle. Hyacinth got out of the taxi and between the excitement of seeing us and looking horrified at where we were, she still managed to say 'Have you stopped shaving under your arms?' Granted, I did need a shave, but a 'hello' would have been nice. I've missed you too.

I saw her take a quick glimpse around and pull a face, as it was backpacker grade and not her usual 54-star. Believe me, this was palatial in comparison to some of the places we had stayed.

Our Hyacinth likes her luxury. A couple of years ago five of us decided to go away for a weekend. Instead of bed and breakfast I rented us a caravan. We could self-cater, the location was great and it was cheap enough, which was what mattered. We arrived and collected the keys for caravan 43A from reception and got directions to the pitch. As we drove around the site we passed some beautiful statics with large decked areas, some with water features and beautiful tended gardens. One in particular had massive double-glazed French windows.

We reached 43A and found a seventies caravan that wouldn't have looked out of place in Beirut. We were hysterical, all except Hyacinth that is. We managed to convince her it wasn't that bad, and after washing it from top to bottom she allowed Vincent to bring her matching Louis Vuitton luggage set in.

5TH FEBRUARY

Newcastle 4, Arsenal 4

Woke up early and had a shave! The heat was stifling, which made the street here absolutely stink. The drains ran under the main street and were only covered by gratings, so the stench was really shocking. At times you had to hold your nose just to walk past.

We enjoyed a day at the beach and afterwards found the duty-free shopping area. The perfume would have actually been cheaper to buy back in the UK, but alcohol was extremely cheap. Newcastle was playing on the television in the evening, so we went off in search of somewhere we could watch it. We passed a large screen and saw that we were getting hammered 4-0 - gutted we were. We decided to walk down on to another stretch of the street and watch it at a small bar up the road, and by the time we got there and watched the end we had managed to get a four-all draw.

Either way we were going to be celebrating or commiserating, so lots of cold beer was on the menu. We decided to stay out to watch the Sunderland v Spurs game, which was kicking off in the early hours of the morning local time. We found a bar where a lad from Sunderland worked. He said a lot of Sunderland fans frequented it and it sometimes got pretty full on match days.

We looked around and saw two other people ordering food. Sunderland was winning but ended up getting beaten by Spurs. So a poor night for Vince but more cold beers for us.

6TH FEBRUARY

From the beach we could see what looked like two huge snow-covered mountains. From here it was pretty difficult to make out what they were, but clearly they couldn't be snow-covered mountains.

We walked along the beach and watched the locals fishing. In the area where the fishermen were sitting was a pile of cigarette ends they had discarded. If they had all got washed into the sea the fish would most probably be suffering from COPD anyway, so a quick hook through its mouth would be the least of its worries. We needed to gatecrash another good hotel. Hyacinth was nearly having a coronary.

Trying to dodge the paragliders that went up every two minutes was a nightmare. One of them crashed into the sand and one into a table, spilling a load of beer and food on to the sand. There were a lot of pissed-off people.

We saw a lad fall from the sky about 15 feet up into the sea, which was only about a metre deep. It looked as if he had either slipped out of the harness or it had snapped. He didn't move at all, and there was mass panic. It was difficult to say if he was dead, but an ambulance was on the scene pretty quickly and he was placed on to a stretcher and taken off. Ten minutes later and they were up and running again. Obviously great health and safety procedures were in place.

7TH FEBRUARY

The rumour had it that the lad didn't die but was seriously injured. We were traumatised after witnessing the disaster, so we gate-crashed the Aseania again. We were welcomed like the regulars we had become. One of the pool attendants even got us four sun-loungers together. One woman was not too pleased as we had our beds next to hers, I think she thought she owned the place. Most of our day was spent sitting in the pool bar drinking. I took great pleasure in knowing I had just peed in the water as she swam past.

At five o' clock the monkeys came down from the mountains and were all sitting round the pool. There were some little baby ones that looked cute until they hissed at you. Apparently they came every night at the same time. I wasn't sure how they knew the time, maybe they had Tony's watch. One in particular looked very guilty, shifty eyes.

I didn't like them and thought they were quite vicious. One in particular took a dislike to Hyacinth and as she leaned in to take a photograph it lunged forward and hissed at her, showing its teeth. We thought it was hilarious, but she wasn't amused. She came out of the pool faster than she would have if she'd been driving a jet ski.

There was a very strange smell nearby, and it seemed to be following me around.

I bumped into my mate who was my sergeant in Newcastle. She was the original Bridget Jones and was now with her husband and their new baby.

8TH FEBRUARY

After arriving at the Aseania we found the pool bar was closed due to refurbishment, so they apologised. Had to do with swimming and sunbathing instead. A terrible inconvenience!

9TH FEBRUARY

We decided to walk up the beach and gatecrash a five-star hotel called the Meritus Pelange Beach Resort. Nothing like a bit of five star when you're backpacking! Hyacinth informed us that this was where she had wanted to stay originally. It was fantastic, with waterfalls, loungers, restaurants, waiters in white suits, the full works, and the pools were beautiful. The prices were ridiculous, so we wouldn't be eating here even if we could (you had to give your room number). It was a bit obvious that we were not staying here as everyone else had green hotel towels, so after a quick walk around I 'acquired' four towels so that we looked as if we belonged.

We had the most amazing day. We decided that when we left we would take the towels with us, so that when we returned we would already have the hotel towels and could come straight in and get a lounger. We were like four asylum seekers doing five stars. There was something great about the fact that we hadn't paid for this but were enjoying it.

10TH FEBRUARY

The Aseania again. I thought I would push my luck and get four towels. When the lad asked me my room number I smiled and said 'if I told you I would have to kill you' and he laughed. I don't think he was bothered, he looked a bit pissed off in his work anyway. The monkeys were late tonight, that's Tony's cheap Benidorm watch for you!

We were chilling out and relaxing at the pool next to a loud-mouthed American bloke (there's no other type, is there?) who was having a conversation with a bloke who looked totally uninterested and embarrassed. Everyone else could hear him, typical. He was telling the other bloke that he thought the Muslims stank and had disgusting habits. Personally I thought he was taking 'freedom of speech' a bit too far. He then told the other bloke that his wife hated him drinking because of his medication. I was tempted to ask him if his medication was preparation H, because he was an arsehole.

11TH FEBRUARY

We went off early in the morning on a three-island boat trip. The first stop was called the 'pregnant ladies' lake', as apparently if you swim in this lake you become pregnant. What a load of crap. There were eighty-year-old women swimming here, unless they had spent too much time in the sun and were only in their thirties. They didn't look capable of carrying their own beach towels, never mind getting pregnant.

Second stop was 'eagle feeding island', pretty self explanatory really – you sit in the boat and throw food into the sea for the eagles to swoop down and feed. They were amazing to watch, though I thought it was a bit sad that instead of them catching their own prey they had it thrown to them without any effort at all. Our Hyacinth thought they just looked like big seagulls.

Final stop was a swimming and snorkelling place. If I never snorkel again I wouldn't miss it. We had to walk quite a distance dodging the monkeys that stood in line and watched us pass. They were like over-confident muggers picking their prey. They let us pass, then swooped and grabbed a bag from a young girl behind us. She screamed and let go and the monkey then ripped her bag open and took her chocolates and sweets out - a monkey with a sweet tooth. Next thing they will be on TV commercials wearing suits and making tea.

I mentioned the monkey and Peter Reid in the same sentence and Vincent decided to take on the monkey, grabbing the bag back from it and whacking it with his towel. At least Vincent was a bit taller than it was. I wasn't sure if he was annoyed or trying to impress the girls, either way the monkey backed down. The walk to the swimming lake was worth it though, and it was fresh water. That strange smell had returned.

12TH FEBRUARY

We went back to the Meritus Pelange equipped with our towels. We no longer looked like four asylum seekers. We choose four good beds and the waiter made sure we were comfortable and then asked if we would like our rooms serviced. I wanted to say 'Yes please, if you go out of here and turn left walk ten minutes up the dirt track and up the road near the laundrette, then it's the first on the right, a little blue door'.

We watched another match – Blackburn 0, Newcastle 0. I love to watch Newcastle on the telly. The cameras scanned over the Blackburn fans and we could see they were all wrapped up in coats, gloves and scarves, it was obviously freezing cold. Then the cameras scanned the Newcastle fans and they were all in their shirts, some were even baring their bare chests. If you're from Newcastle you will know it is an offence to wear a coat in any conditions, especially freezing temperatures, so the Toon Fans are used to it.

14TH FEBRUARY

I woke up at four o clock in the morning, not because it was Valentine's Day but because of the early start in the mosque, which is four times a day now at four am, nine am, two pm and six pm. It's testing my patience and I am beginning to have nervous twitches. It's driving me mad. I just don't understand why they have to blast it out of massive speakers. I mean, if Allah can see and hear everything he already knows they're praying.

We watched another match in our local bar on the beach - Newcastle 2, Birmingham 0.

15TH FEBRUARY

We decided to be brave today and go up the mountain in the cable car to see the two huge 'snow-covered mountains'. It wasn't until we got to the top that we found out that they were actually lookout stations, and it was the white canopies we could see. Going up on the cable car was terrifying, it was so far up you couldn't even imagine how high. If you said 1000 cars piled on top of each other you still wouldn't be close. It was worth it when we got to the top though, and on the way up it was quite satisfying to see my sister being terrified and clawing into Vincent's arm because of the shaving comment.

At the top there was a huge suspension bridge which was terrifying, you could feel it swaying. It was so high that the trees underneath looked like broccoli. I must admit I only went so far then turned back, as did our Sharron, but Tony and Vince walked the whole lot.

When we got back down to earth (literally) we called into Raffi's bar on the beach, and then a huge storm came. There were people running for cover and jet skis coming back into land quicker than they had gone out. We just got in on time. Fancy getting 'rained in' at a pub, it was like a dream come true for Tony and me. It's what you wish for all your life. Remember when you were a kid and you would point at a sweet shop and say 'Imagine getting locked in there all night, what would you do?' Girls always used to say 'I would eat all the chocolate'.

We started talking to a group of Indian blokes, good crack, I showed them a few tricks. I did think about showing them the one I picked up in Thailand but I didn't have any ping pong balls, so that's another story! Instead I showed them how to make a chicken out of a tea towel. They were easily pleased. Anyway it made them laugh and I got a free beer.

One of the men from the group told us about some of the Indian traditions, which were fascinating. He told us that a coloured spot on the forehead of a lady means she is married, while a black spot signifies she is still single, although you don't see this one very often. Maybe it's only used on the ugly ones, given that a huge percentage are arranged marriages anyway and let's face it you would have to hate someone to make them marry an ugly bride. A yellow or gold spot means 'from the Gods', although I wasn't sure what he meant by that. A toe ring signifies being married (to us it's just fashion). At

Hong Kong scenery

Bangkok street seller

Steph with a tiger, Thailand

Elephants in Chang Rai, Thailand

Rural Bangkok, Bangplee Yai area

Steph with tiger cub in Chang Mai, Thailand

Tony working in the fields, Chang Rai, Thailand

With a local village boy, Chang Rai, Thailand

Children in their house, Chang Rai, Thailand

View of the village, Chang Rai, Thailand

Walking street, Pattaya, Thailand

Steph on the beach swing, Ko Samet, Thailand

Ko Samet beach, Thailand

Our friends the cockroaches

Dinner of cockroaches

The local pub, Hanoi, Vietnam

Halong Bay

Ming Mang Tomb, Vietnam

Ho Ann Island, Vietnam

Ho Chi Minh Mausoleum, Vietnam

Quy Nhon, Vietnam

Quy Nhon, Vietnam

Christmas Day on the beach, Nh Trang, Vietnam

With a street seller, Nh Trang, Vietnam

Our tree room, Vietnam

Christmas in Na Trang, Vietnam

Saigon traffic, Vietnam

Dish of snails, Vietnam

Cambodian housing

Tony and Steph in Phuket, Thailand

Killing Fields, Cambodia

The main street in Sihanoukville, Cambodia

The restaurant in Sihanoukville

Angkor Wat, Cambodia

Angkor Thom, Cambodia

Steph arriving in Malaysia

Hawkers Centre, Malaysia

Deserted beach, Malaysia

The pool bar, Asenia Hotel, Langkawi, Malaysia

Pelangi beach resort, Langkawi, Malaysia

Singapore hostel

Singapore hostel

With a kangaroo in Cudlee Creek, Adelaide

Kangaroos

Our hippy camper van

Feeding the wild parrots

The floods after the creek broke its bank

Tony in the floods

One of the 1930s shacks built during the depression

Sydney Bridge and Harbour

Termite hill, New South Wales, Australia

North Island scenery, New Zealand

Chile, Santiago

Cusco, Peru

Milford Sound, South Island

Mirror Lake, South Island

Fox Glacier, South Island

Hokitika Gorge, South Island

Rotorua. North Island

Maori girl, North Island

Chile, South America

Vina Del Mar

Bar Sifflus, Vina del Mar

Abandoned cemetery, Atacama Desert

Andes Mountains, Atacama Desert

Hand of the Desert, Atacama Desert

Abandoned trains, Atacama Desert

Luna Valley (Moon Valley), Atacama Desert

San Pedro, Atacama Desert

Cusco, Peru

Machu Picchu

Christ the Redeemer, Rio

The famous steps in Rio

A favela in Rio

the wedding reception they spread rice and salt in each other's hair (I suppose if you got pissed at the reception you would always have something to eat in bed). The females wear their wedding ring on their third finger left hand and the men third finger right hand. A woman will often wear a ring on a chain around her neck so that it is always near her heart.

As this bloke was telling me this he was slowly getting more and more intoxicated. He thought Hyacinth was from the gods, as she never touches alcohol. I asked if his wife was allowed to drink and he said only if she prayed afterwards. I thought to myself, if that was me I'd have to have carpet fitters' pads constantly fitted on my knees.

As we were having this interesting conversation I heard my sister telling one of the other blokes that she had been to Copenhagen. Later I asked her when she had been to Copenhagen. She said

'When we were in London we went.'

'Did we?' I said

'Yes, it's in London.'

'Is it?'

'A think so.'

Thankfully she had nothing to do with our route map.

16TH FEBRUARY

We called for breakfast at our little local breakfast bar, then headed down to the Meritus Pelange to have some five-star luxuries again. On arrival we spread our green hotel towels on four loungers. We saw a couple of lads who had been in the same breakfast place as us and were walking around the pool looking for loungers and spotted us. They made out like they hadn't seen us and disappeared. They must have thought we would shop them for not being residents. They probably thought we were, given that we had hotel towels.

As I lay on the sun bed I spotted little ants and threw tiny pieces of biscuit for them and watched them carrying it away. They can carry something like ten times their own body weight, isn't that amazing? Well I have news for you, we have wagons, so fuck you ants.

We now have two towels each, so we might try and get the matching dressing gowns and slippers tomorrow.

17TH FEBRUARY

We had pretty much the same day today. A bit of five star never did anyone any harm, plus we had to leave our towels (you didn't think we were keeping them did you, that would be theft) as we wouldn't be back so we didn't need them any more. Neither did we have any need for dressing gowns and slippers. Anyway Tony and I might become targets of jealous backpackers in our hostels, so we didn't bother.

Tony and Vince went off for a pint and Hyacinth and I were having a fish foot spa, it was only £2 here (£20 at home). It felt strange at first, like millions of tiny mild electric shocks, but it was good. Afterwards we had a foot massage, which was just a way to dry our feet really, nothing special.

As we were leaving we bumped into a couple we had met in Penang who were also backpacking. They stayed at the Muslim home with us, but they had a proper room, not one made of plywood and sticky-back plastic.

18TH FEBRUARY

We got up at 6 am to see Sharron and Vince off. We then travelled to the ferry terminal, where we caught a ferry back into Thailand and headed up by local bus to Phuket. We stopped at a place called Patong, which was mad busy with every bar and club you could imagine. The beach was not as nice as I thought, but it's so busy it would probably never look like paradise.

We had booked into the Blue Sea guest house for two nights. We always booked our hostels for two nights, then if we liked it we could stay and if it was crap we could move on. It was spot on, clean, on a quiet street with everything we needed, so we negotiated a deal with the landlady and in typical Thai tradition she tried to rip us off by telling us the room cost more for more nights, and then showed us the other room at our price.

She showed us up four flights of stairs to room 999 (no joke) and opened the door and pointing inside said 'for dinna'. She was pointing to an enormous table in the middle of the room. It was big enough to serve a whole cow and seat about twelve people. I don't know what she thought we ate. The imitation leather sofas looked like they had been refurbished by Edward Scissorhands. We politely said no thanks and told her we wanted the room we were in. After twenty minutes of haggling we got to stay where we were. We were more than pleased because we had a fridge, television, DVD en suite and a massive balcony, all for £6 a night each.

To celebrate our victory we hit the town, full-on lights, glitz and glamour, and that was just the ladyboys. The downside to this is you get ripped off, the entertainment is great but the prices and the beer are shit. After checking out the various bars, and there were too many to mention in this area, we found a nice little place to eat off the main street. It was full of Thais, so we knew it was going to be good.

20TH FEBRUARY

It was roasting hot again. We headed to the beach and made it our mission to find a space on the sand big enough for two beach towels. After a little while we found a spot. We watched the sellers going up and down the beach targeting the new arrivals. They work the beach so often they know who's just arrived. We were very tanned now, so we didn't get much hassle as it looked like we had been here a long time.

A woman was settling on a price to have her feet massaged. I don't think she bartered enough. You could tell she liked to be pampered and liked lying in the sun. She had a chest like corrugated brown cardboard.

22ND FEBRUARY

Again the weather started off a bit overcast, but within an hour the sun had broken through and it was blistering hot again. We were in a bar and Sky News came on, saying there had been an earthquake in Christchurch New Zealand, which was pretty scary as we were flying there in a month's time. We had so far managed to either be in front of or behind every disaster that had occurred so we hoped it would stay that way.

We decided to go into town to see the action, and within an hour we were offered a choice of 'special massage for two', 'special massage for one', 'special massage with two girls' and the special 'ping pong show'. No matter how special they were, we declined all of them in the quest for cheap beer.

We were dragged into a bar by a 6ft Lola and 'she' insisted on bringing us two pints of lager. Tony's face was tripping him up as he had just noticed the price of the beer, which in our money was about £3 a pint (ridiculous for Thailand). Lola was quickly back with the beers balanced on a tray. You had to admire 'her' being on her feet all night in those killer heels. Tony's face was still tripping him.

Our drinks were put on the table and as Lola stretched over, her large silicone breast carefully brushed against Tony's shoulder, which brought a smile to his face (although he will tell you it didn't, it was wind). I think Lola liked it too, because when she walked away she gave Tony a huge smile. He smiled back, the wind again.

Tony looked at his pint and said 'That's crap, it's flat' so I shouted Lola over. Smiling and pointing at Tony, I said to Lola he would like some head. Tony nearly choked on his flat pint, but I enjoyed watching him squirm. I thought, that will teach you for your face tripping you up all night.

After quite a while of enjoying Tony trying to explain that he wanted a head on his pint and not what Lola was thinking (and hoping, I think), he settled for his flat pint. The whole night was quite surreal, as we tried to spot the real and the fake women. We spotted a 6ft nun, or should I say she spotted us and walked up to Tony with her hands clasped together in a prayer sign and started singing 'I will swallow you' (it was a hymn I wasn't familiar with, but the tune I knew).

As we watched Lola walk away with her tiny little bum squeezed into a pair of trousers that Olivia Newton John would have been proud of, I heard me mother's voice in my head saying 'you're big-boned our Stephanie, you're just big-boned'. Someone then shouted to Lola 'Hey, have you always had big tits', and Lola shouted 'No, you're my first'.

23RD FEB 2011

We went to a little bar facing our hostel and had the biggest breakfast I had ever seen in my life. We ate far too much and then headed off to the beach, where we had to sit like a couple of beached whales. Tony was fascinated at the way the young lads wore their Calvin Klein underpants above their swimming shorts, so you could read the lettering. Above the letters were their sun-tanned six packs.

Now because I know Tony so well I knew what he was thinking. I told him I didn't really think the under-the-nipple look with Jockey showing round the waistband would catch on.

We spent the afternoon watching people on the beach, pretending to be asleep when the sellers were going past and watching the behaviour of the girls jumping up to wipe sand off themselves or rearrange their beach towels when the lads went past. We watched the lads nudging each other when the girls went past.

After a while we got bored so we went off for a walk. Tony was still blaming me for his stomach-ache and said it was the beer last night. He needed the toilet, so we went into a little bar and ordered a drink. We realised that the bar did not have a toilet of its own. Tony asked and was told there was a toilet that several of the bars use and it was just up the lane. What they didn't tell him was that it was about ten bars away and it was a squat job with no toilet roll. Tony came back and said to the girl behind the bar: 'There's no toilet roll.'

'Ah, you find toilet' she said.

'Yes but there's no toilet roll.'

'I show you where toilet is, come with me.'

'No I know where it is, I've been but there's no paper.'

'You know where it is?'

'Yes.'

'And you use?'

'No.'

'No, I confused, why you not use, you said you want to go?'

'Yes I know.'

'But you not use?'

'There's no toilet roll!'

'I show you where to go.'

'I know where to go, but there's no toilet paper.'

'I not understand.'

'Toilet, no paper, just toilet.'

'Well go then.'

'I don't want to go.'

'But you asked for toilet.'

'Yes but with toilet roll!'

By this time it was like a Morecambe and Wise sketch and I couldn't drink my pint for laughing.

'Solly I no understand you.'

'No toilet paper, man.'

'You want man?'

'No, I want the toilet with some fucking toilet paper in it.'

At last the barman says 'Ah no toilet paper' then goes into hysterics 'No paper, ha ha ha ha ha ha!'

It's now like the sketch from Trains, Planes and Automobiles at the car hire desk. By now the whole bar is watching and I don't know who's more embarrassed, Tony who's shitting himself, or me who's watching.

By this time Tony had resigned himself to the fact that he was wasting his time and had sat on the bar stool next to me. A little Thai fella spied his Rolex Oyster watch and pointed to it, asking 'is this real?'

'Why aye it's real, all the way from Cambodia' Tony said.

The Thai fella laughed and got out a big bag of leather wallets which he then placed all over the bar. Tony told him he wasn't interested, but the bloke insisted. He got out a bag of sunglasses and the same thing happened. He put them on Tony and then a pair on me. 'Try these ones, velly good for too much light.' He put them on the counter and again we said we weren't interested. After several bags of glasses, belts, wallets, caps, bracelets and T shirts he said 'Please you buy one thing from me, what you like, I sell you.'

Tony said 'How much is a toilet roll?'

Even the barman laughed.

We headed off for a walk and to take in some of the 'culture' after the toilet roll episode, which was never resolved. We had to then find another bar, and this time Tony checked for toilet roll before he bought the drinks.

It's an eye opener to say the least when you see the blokes parading their 'girlfriends' on their arm. They walk as if to say 'Look at this gorgeous girl I scored with'. I think, no, you bought her, because you're fat, old and ugly and no woman in her right mind would want to be seen with you. They parade them up and down not realising how pathetic and sad they look. They all say things like 'She said I'm not like all the others, she said I'm different, she really likes me, she lives with her mother who needs £200 for new teeth and says she feels terrible taking the money off me, I'm going to send her £300 a month until she can sort out her visa and we can be together and live happily ever after in the Byker Wall (bog standard housing) or somewhere just as nice! She says she's not bothered where we live as long as we're together.' The sad reality is that she would bomb him out for his father if he paid more.

On we went in search of more 'culture' and passed a live entertainment bar, where we watched for a while. They were running a singing competition, and to say it was bad would be an understatement. It was hardly X Factor. Danni would have said 'Thanks but it's not for me'. Louis would have giggled his way through it, then said 'You know what Simon it's not all about you, I think he has something special. I like him and I'm gonna say yes'. Cheryl would have said 'A like yer, ya a bit oot a tune at times but yi kna what, it's hard, av bin there but ye bring fun to the competition and that's what it's all aboot so am ganna say yis'. Simon would have said 'Well I don't know what these two idiots are watching but it's not the same as me, you were out of tune and you would be better off going back to your day jobs because you're never going to make it in the pop world'. Boos all round to which Simon backs down, only to discover the new Backward, the answer to Jedward.

We took a slow walk back to our hostel, where we had the added luxury of an en-suite toilet and toilet roll on tap. I wish I knew what the smell was though, it's still following me around.

We got into reception and asked for the key. The lady then said to Tony 'you have wankey?'. Tony looked at me with a look on his face that was exactly the same as mine, until the penny dropped and we both realised she had meant, do you only have one key.

Toilet episode over, thank the lord, but no doubt there will be many more instances like this one.

Have you ever heard yourself on holiday? When you speak to other people not from England you describe things that are completely untrue but you actually believe them at the time. I'm not sure what it is, whether it's the weather or you just get wound up in the moment.

We say things like 'Oh in England we never get sunshine, only rain, snow, and cold. If we're lucky we'll get two days of sunshine in one week, which we call our summer. Last winter it was minus 10 every night, very very cold, need lots of winter clothing.' Which is also all said in broken English, whether the person speaks perfect English or not. Now correct me if I'm wrong but I could have just described David Attenborough's Antarctica. Another thing is that we all think it is compulsory to indulge in the full English breakfast, when at home we would be happy with a bowl of snap crackle and pop, and Bob's your uncle, unless you live in Middlesbrough, then he would be your uncle, dad and brother, but that's another story.

24TH FEBRUARY

Took the local taxi to Karon Beach, which was a lot nicer than Patong Beach, apart from the fact that people insisted on smoking and leaving their fag ends all over. I would have liked to shove their fag ends up their arses, but the prospect of a spell in the Bangkok Hilton did not appeal to me.

We stopped off for a beer on the way back and had the pleasure of watching a fat old bloke with his fingers probing inside the shorts of a young woman as she mopped the sweat off his Bobby Charlton haircut and kissed his fat sweaty neck. I bet she couldn't wait to be in the Byker Wall with the man of her dreams.

25TH FEBRUARY

On walking down to the beach this morning I played with the idea of buying a paper until I saw the headline on a redtop, 'how the fox did he get up there?' which related to a story about a fox that somehow managed to get to the top of the Shard Tower in London, the tallest building in England. Never mind that New Zealand was counting its dead. I wasn't missing the English tabloids.

There was a lot going on at the beach with jet skis, banana rides and paragliding, all of which I had participated in at least once during some holiday. I would never recommend riding on the banana. After the tenth time of falling off and a lad who looked like he was about fourteen and about six and a half stone had had to lift me back on, I vowed I would never put anyone through that trauma again. I keep on waiting for a 'where there's blame there's a claim' letter to fall on the mat from a paraplegic in Thailand. When I think back we actually did a double paraglide for our honeymoon, with Tony strapped on to my back - mind you we were a lot slimmer then.

There was lots going on in the bars on Bangla Road. It was only two o' clock and already the girls were helping the men to part with their hard-earned cash. 'I love you long time' she says as she snuggles up to his fat hairy sweaty chest. Yeah sure you do, next thing he knows her mother needs new teeth and the dad's in hock with the local gangster and he's about to be beheaded if he doesn't send her two hundred quid a month. Yeah, she really loves you!

Down the road was a bar called 'Love you short time', and I'm not joking. You can't get fairer that that I suppose.

There was a lad sitting in a bar strumming his guitar, which reminded me of Christmas at my brother's house. My nephews Jack and Ben (AKA Ronnie and Reggie) were calling the bingo numbers for our after-dinner entertainment (it's all go at ours!) when Ben decided to give us a number on his guitar. So he sat on the chair and started to play, and sounded shit by the way (I don't believe in telling kids they're great when they are clearly not, they have to learn the hard way, life's not meant to be easy). Five minutes later he went off for a drink. When he came back he played the guitar using his other hand. I said to him 'Ben, you had the guitar in the other hand before' and he said 'Yes well it all depends which chair the teacher sits me on if there's room for me to get my guitar in'. Needless to say my brother cancelled his lessons when he heard that. Ben was no Eric Clapton, so nothing lost. Anyway it made light entertainment having an ambidextrous bingo caller.

We went into a bar on the beach, and I know it's hard to comprehend but I was having a diet coke, which made me think about how I was speaking. I was saying 'can I get' instead of 'can I have'. It made me think of my mother, who would be speaking in a mixture of accents by now, so no one would be able to pin point where she was from. Some people live away all their lives and don't really change, and others just pick up accents everywhere they go. If my mother goes to Scotland for two days she comes back with a Scots accent. My brother lives in Northumberland, where there is a much defined accent where people roll their R's. My nephew asked 'Nanna, can you roll your R's?' to which my mother put her hands on her hips and gyrated her rear. Needless to say my nephew was confused. Sometimes you don't know if it's the accent or she just gets the words mixed up, she still says Lady Di was killed by MFI.

26TH FEBRUARY

At the beach this morning I bumped into an old friend from training school - it's a small world. I told him to watch out for petty criminals, especially the shirt lifter robbers, the ones that take you from behind. Yes, I have been on several diversity courses, but that one still makes me laugh.

Next to us on the beach I couldn't take my eyes off two lads and a girl who had had so much Botox they looked like they were made of plastic. I bet when they got told the price they couldn't even look shocked. They look hideous. She was like the bride of Frankenstein. It was like a freak show on the beach.

Behind the Botox Three was a woman having her hair braided, and by the way she was smiling she was very pleased. She looked like bloody Stevie Wonder, with multi-coloured beads threaded into hundreds of plaits. Mind you, it's not fair that men in their eighties can wear shorts and vests and look great while women who dress a bit younger can just look so wrong.

'I just called to say I love you' is nearly finished and looks ridiculous. If the wind whips up she could have some serious lacerations on her face.

Today we found out that all the noise and excitement in the street was Gay Pride. It was incredible. I challenge any bloke to pick the men from the girls out here, they are absolutely beautiful. The first of loads of floats started to go past, and it appeared that Priscilla Queen of the Desert was on them all. All the floats had a theme – we even saw a leather float go by. I never saw so many men grabbing the camera and taking pictures. The foam float passed and then it was the Kings and Queens float. There was a distinct lack of kings though, they were all queens. The floats just kept on coming. It was the best carnival I had ever seen.

We hit our little local bar at the corner of our street because it's pretty quiet, and watched another match, Newcastle 1 - Bolton 1. We met a lad in there originally from Gateshead, Tyne and Wear, but now living in Singapore and on holiday in Thailand. He told us about a bar in Singapore that was Toon barmy, we knew we'd have to take a look when we were there.

The atmosphere for the match was great, shame it was only a draw. The Thai girls from the bar took pity on us and bought us some roasted cockroaches as a treat. Personally I would have been happy with a pint or a packet of KP dry roasted, but it was nice of them. They told us that these cockroaches were pretty expensive as they were imported from Vietnam and Laos because they were nice and big! They cost 30 baht for three, which is about eighty pence, so I suppose they were quite costly. Anyway they had bought them for us, so the lesson in eating them began. First place it in your hand (it filled my hand), then turn it over so it's face down. Next crush the shell and scoop the meat out with your finger and enjoy, like a crab. Well to say I wouldn't recommend them is an understatement, but when in Rome. I thought mine tasted like rotten seaweed and Tony thought his was like beef, which made a change because usually everything tastes like chicken.

27TH FEBRUARY

Had my feet done today at the fish spa. There are apparently 1000 fish in each tank and don't you just know that some tosser was there trying to count them. A bit like the ten-year old geek who counts the contents of a box of Rice Krispies, then writes to the manufactures to inform them that they are wrong and that it is false advertising. Wouldn't you just love it if some director had the balls to write back and say:

Dear Timothy,

I am in receipt of your sad pathetic letter dated 27th Feb 2011 regarding the number of 'snap crackle and pops' in the average spoonful.

You should learn not to take things so literally as it makes you sound like the sad little geeky fucker that you are. You mention you have a brother and have enclosed a photograph of your family. My first reaction on seeing your mother was total shock that someone would shag her twice, but after seeing your retard of a father I now understand. I am so glad that your parents have not split up as it would be a waste of two houses. I suggest you drag yourself away from your computer games and stop trying to master the art of masturbation, as you will have plenty of time to do that when you remain single for the rest of your sad pathetic life as the little fuckwit that you quite evidently are.

Yours sincerely

The very highly-paid boss of 'who gives a fuck how many snap crackle and pop's there are in a box' company.

PS Get a fucking life.

Walked up the road and looked for a nice place to stop off for a drink. Declined the offer of the first drink on account of the waitress's mustard yellow teeth, it's not exactly someone you want at front of house is it? If you can't look after your teeth then you aren't going to be that bothered about the state of the glasses or anything else. We opted for next door.

28TH FEBRUARY

We checked out of our hostel and caught the local bus from Patong through Thung Thong to Phuket town. We were on the bus for what seemed like an eternity, but there were plenty of interesting characters getting on and off, so it kept our interest levels high. There was everyone from old ladies carrying fish (or that's what it smelt like anyway) to girls dressed to the nines looking like they were going night clubbing but obviously going to 'work'. The bus cost us 25 bhat each, but it would have been 400 in a taxi so good housekeeping done there.

We arrived back in the land of the cockroach, and the roaches here were like small gerbils, bloody horrible things. Not much going on in the town as it was mainly away from the tourist trap, so when we found a nice little Italian place and went inside. It's easier to sit inside as it reduces the sightings of cockroaches. Once inside we noticed that we were the only people in, apart from the table in the corner which looked like it was being occupied by the family of the restaurant.

The restaurant was a very authentic-looking place with a stereotypical Italian mother sitting with her three sons and two of the wife's. The mother looked like the kind of woman who would wash the inside of her son's car after he had murdered someone, then say 'My boy, he was home all night with his mamma'. Either way when the pizza came I was eating it no questions asked. It was pretty poor, but we didn't complain. After what seemed like fourteen hours of chewing the mozzarella on the top I was full.

1ST MARCH

My jaw still ached this morning from the mozzarella. We had booked into a small hostel up a back lane along the road from the Pink Palace, and when we asked for directions we were told to ask for the Pink Palace, because when you get to the Pink Palace you can see the hostel. We didn't know what the Pink Palace was until we arrived. It was only the next day, after getting laughed and sneered at, that we found out that it was a lap-dancing place with 'extras'.

We had breakfasted with six other guests of the hostel. We were lucky because the French had to speak English if they couldn't speak Thai. They were quite rude, so it was what they deserved.

Outside our hostel was a piece of wasteland where there was a house occupied by a family. They appeared to be living quite happily and were self-sufficient with their small garden, where they were growing vegetables. It was very roughly made of corrugated sheeting and a couple of old doors. It reminded me of the first leek trench my dad made in our back garden, right under the sitting room window. Every week my dad would pour leek feed and some dead animal's blood all over it. The smell was hideous, but that year he won a bathroom cabinet so all of a sudden it made it all worthwhile.

As we walked past they spotted us and shouted sawadeeka, which is 'hello' in Thai. They offered us drinks and huge smiles and showed us their garden. The man of the house was telling me that he had to feed his crop and I was tempted to ask if the Italian restaurant mother supplied him with the blood, but thought I'd better not. It raises the question 'who's the richest?' They had huge hearts, great values, great morals and nothing materialistic. They also made shit juice, but the thought was nice.

Chapter Eight

SINGAPORE

2ND MARCH

We had to be up early this morning to catch our flight to Singapore. We got to the airport with loads of time to spare, so we had a cursory check to make sure we had no chewing gum in our bags (chewing gum is banned in Singapore). Despite getting there early and getting checked in, we were not given seats together.

After boarding the flight and getting comfortable it became apparent that the plane was not full, so we could move seats and sit together after all. Was it possible that while they were booking on the passengers for the flight they deliberately separated people to spread the weight around the plane? After several people did the same as us I was worried that we would fly around in circles.

We eventually landed in Singapore. The airport was manic and massive, and after we had cleared customs for the umpteenth time it was time to study our map again to see where we needed to be next. After great deliberation we agree that we needed to be on the Skytrain going north to our hostel. We were staying outside Singapore, as it was too expensive to stay in the city centre. We were on the train for two minutes and found that we were going in the right direction, so all was looking good. The train was full, so we had to stand all the way.

After an hour and a half we got to our stop. We were told to get off the train, walk straight ahead and at the park look right, and we would see the hostel, which was in a block of flats (in the middle of a concrete jungle). We did all that and there in front of our eyes we both saw the hostel. You couldn't miss it. The front door was bright orange and the gate was purple. We assumed that because it was in the middle of a block of flats they had used the colours to help people find the place.

We rang the buzzer and waited a few minutes until the door was opened by a small Chinese lady. We immediately went into fits of laughter when we saw inside the hostel. I had never seen anything like it. We were shown up a flight of stairs, and it was beginning to feel like we had dropped an acid tablet. The stairs had been hand-painted lime green, orange, purple, red, yellow and blue. On the wall was a full-size stuffed alligator.

When we reached the top of the stairs we saw a huge room containing twelve bunk beds. A few were occupied with various rucksacks and stuff, so we opted for the quieter corner. There was a little fella lying on his bed, and when he spoke we nearly died as we hadn't even noticed him there.

He started telling us that nothing was how it appeared. Confused and still in shock from the bright colours, Tony said 'What do you mean?' I was hoping he wasn't going to ask because I had visions of us being murdered in our beds (and our blood being sold off for leek trenches). He repeated again in a Peter Cushing voice 'Everything you see is not what you think'. I was thinking 'too right, it looks OK on the internet'.

Then we found out what he meant. The chairs around the table were actually toilets, the fridge was the wardrobe, the wardrobe was the fridge, the stools were empty cable reels and the kitchen roll dispenser was an old fax machine. I had visions of Rolf sketching away now saying 'Can yer tell what it is yit?' 'Er no Rolf, we're not even warm'.

Colin and Justin would have had a fit. But overall the hostel was OK, and cleanish. It seemed friendly enough and it certainly gave you something to talk about. I could smell that smell again.

We picked our bunks, left our rucksacks and went out to check out the local area. It looked OK, but there wasn't much around except a couple of local indoor market-type places which were great for somewhere to eat and get a drink.

3RD MARCH

Neither of us slept much during that first night in Singapore. The bloody fans were on all night because of the heat. I thought at one point I was sleeping in a helipad and was going to be blown off the bed, only to land with my fingers and toenails stuck in the wall alongside the alligator. I had visions of being used as a tea towel holder. Don't imagine it for too long, will you.

Mr H was ordered off the top bunk due to a weight restriction. He's not that heavy but I imagine the weight restriction here is quite low as the Singaporeans all have 26-inch waists and weigh in at about seven stone each. There is only so much weight an aluminium bunk bed can bear.

We caught the train into Singapore city and found it was beautiful. It was a huge place with lots of skyscrapers, and in the centre loads of green areas and parks. We walked through the town and to the Boat Quay area, which was mega expensive and gorgeous.

We checked out the bar that the lad in Thailand had told us to go and see. It was called the Penny Black and was covered in Toon Army memorabilia. They even had a Singapore Magpies crest (Newcastle United). Anyone visiting Singapore who is a Newcastle fan should definitely have a look. It's at the foot of the tallest building in Singapore, so you can't fail to find it - just ask for directions. I swear it's nowhere near the Pink Palace.

The streets were beautiful, no graffiti or litter anywhere and the whole place was gleaming clean. But there is always one I suppose. We were happily sitting watching the boats on the river and trying to imagine their value when a scruffy-looking bloke with a manky guitar strapped over his shoulder threw his sandwich in the river. It's such an affluent area that even the tramps can afford to throw their sandwiches away. I called him a right merchant banker, but Tony said he wasn't because he didn't have a suit on.

There were two huge skyscrapers next to one another and on top of them was a full-size ship that was probably a posh restaurant. It looked incredible, the mind boggled as to how they had done it. I did take some pictures but the smog made it hard to appreciate how magnificent it was.

The sky suddenly went totally black and there was a massive clap of thunder. Lightning lit up the sky and people were running for cover. We ran into a bar and were gutted at the six-quid-a-pint price tag, but had one anyway. It was probably the most expensive pint I have ever had in my life, and I have realised that there is an art in sipping a pint. It's not worth it. Just drink it and enjoy it.

The storm went on for nearly two hours, so we were forced to have another beer. When the rain subsided we went to Raffles to take a look, but didn't bother with the Singapore Sling.

4TH MARCH

We checked out of the hostel and went off to the zoo. We are not lovers of zoos, but Singapore's is pretty incredible. We really wanted to spend some time with the orang-utans in the wild, but because it's quite difficult to see them we opted for the ones at the zoo. They are free range and are literally above your head, and will reach down and touch your hand, it's amazing.

I was taking a photo of one, Clyde, when he became curious and reached down for the camera. As one of his 'in laws' had Tony's watch I wasn't taking any chances with my camera. Clyde then came down to have his picture taken, but there was no sign of Clint, more's the pity. I wanted to take one home, but Tony said he wasn't taking it for a walk and cleaning up after it, so I would have to leave him here (the orang-utan, not Tony). Clyde would probably be less trouble looking after.

We spent all day at the zoo and it was magnificent. We then had to catch three trains to get to the airport to fly to our next country - Australia.

Tony took advantage of the free Wifi while I was busy scanning the people to see who was potentially going to be sitting next to me. I saw a lady who I think starred in 'Throw mamma from the train' and several Bruce Lee lookalikes. I played with the idea of holding a sick bag open when I sat down in the hope that no one would sit next to me.

The toilets were posh, and after you use the loo there's a system that blows you dry - good or what? That's probably why the queue for the men's is so long, someone obviously came back and said 'Hey, you get a free blow job in there'. Tony had already been and was tickled by the idea, so when I came back he said 'Did you get your bits blown?' in his usual ninety-decibel voice. At least twenty people were sitting looking at me and waiting for my reply. I couldn't decide whether to own up to the old-fashioned technique of a bit of toilet roll or admit I had gone for the cut and blow dry look. I said nothing and sat down smiling through gritted teeth.

We got on to the plane, and as requested Mr H had his window seat and I had two empty seats next to me. Result! When the waitress came she asked me what I would like to drink and I pointed to the empty seats and said 'wine please, and my two friends will have the same'. She obviously knew the seats were empty but laughed and brought them anyway, another result.

Tony had gone to the toilet, so I thought I had better order for him. The lady asked me what he would like and I thought about saying 'Well, the only thing he doesn't drink is petrol' but I ordered him a Jack Daniels and Coke. She must have read my mind, because she brought him a double.

Chapter Nine

AUSTRALIA

5TH MARCH 2011

Today we arrived in Australia. After declaring our small amount of foodstuffs on the paperwork we were given on the plane, we were allowed through with very little hassle. I thought they would have you empty your bags and everything after what I had seen on the television, but I was wrong.

We came out of the airport and caught the local bus to our hostel in Adelaide. We were there within about forty minutes. Our room at the hostel was very small with bunk beds. We could have had another five nights in Asia for the price of this hostel - it was £40 a night.

But Adelaide looked nice enough. We dumped our stuff and went out to explore what was on offer. The city's biggest shopping mall is the Rundle, beside the river Torrens. The whole place was alive with stalls and street performers, because it was the fringe festival. There were numerous street entertainments, along with the Aborigines who sell their original artwork on the street. Some of it was quite nice, but it was an acquired taste.

We arranged to meet my mate Andy, who I had worked with during my policing days. He was in Adelaide on his career break and policing Adelaide for five years. This evening he came and picked us up and we had a BBQ at his house. We tried kangaroo meat. Tony liked it, but I'm not a massive meat eater. Personally I preferred the BBQ sauce, and anyway I have a soft spot for kangaroos.

We went to the off-licence and took a carry-out of lager, £35 for a case, ouch. Andy's house was up a hill, so on the drive back we could see the city all lit up.

6TH MARCH

Five minutes' walk from our hostel we were right in the centre of town. The weather was red hot, so the festival was going great. We sat for ages watching a magic act - I don't usually like this type of thing but it captured my imagination for a while. We visited the famous Haige's Chocolate Shop and got some free samples. I was glad we got some freebies because it was very expensive.

7TH MARCH

Andy came to pick us up and we went to a place called Cudlee Creek. Andy's mother was visiting, so she came with us. They had an area where kangaroos, wallabies and koalas live. We got to hold a koala, which was lovely, it just clung on to me for a cuddle, and it had soft fur and held on to a eucalyptus leaf which it was eating constantly. They apparently eat eucalyptus all day and are consequently 'stoned'. I'm not sure if it would work for humans or not. No doubt someone somewhere will try, but if it opens the flood gates (because I don't think it is classed as a drug), imagine all the eucalyptus trees that would be planted.

8TH MARCH

I never slept a bloody wink after developing an allergy to the sheets, or rather what they had been washed in. My skin was red raw, and I had to get out the silk sleeping bag that I had taken to use in

Asia in case the beds weren't clean. I never thought I would be using it in Australia. I was so glad I had brought it.

It was pouring with rain today but still hot. I love watching the rain when you don't have to go out anywhere. Tony and several others had taken an interest in two girls who were in the kitchen during breakfast. They were openly kissing and touching each other. One lad was supposed to be reading his book, but he never turned a page. One of the girls said 'shall ve take another shower?' in a broken accent as she nuzzled into the other one's neck, either not bothered as to who was spectating or oblivious. Everyone was now looking and suddenly didn't seem to care what was for tea. This went on for about ten minutes, until they decided to head off to their room.

The men in the room seemed to be using a secret language known only to other men, which didn't require words. They were grinning at each other and looking very pleased with themselves.

9TH MARCH

Tony got up early this morning to check out, as he said, the 'lesbians', and he was not disappointed. He came back saying they must be the cleanest lesbians in Adelaide, because they were in the shower again. He brought me a cup of tea and for some reason he had put sugar in mine. I have never taken sugar, so I wonder what it was that distracted him so much!

We checked out of the hostel and caught a local bus to the airport, where we flew to Melbourne and picked up a camper van. We arrived at the camper van place to be shown a 'Hippy Van' - it was great. It had pink and purple flowers all over it. It was tiny inside, so that was going to be a lot of fun.

Once the van had been checked over and we had been given a quick guide as to how everything worked, which took all of ten minutes given the size of it, we were given the green light. We didn't have a clue where we were going, but we had picked up a map with the camper and headed off in the direction of Sydney. We had never been here anyway, so wherever we ended up was going to be a bonus.

Our first stop was the bottle shop, which was a drive-through, like a cash and carry where you buy your beers and wines. You can only buy them here as not all the supermarkets sell alcohol. I treated myself to a four-litre box of rosé wine and Tony got a couple of cases of beer. This took up practically all the space we had in the camper.

The drive along the coast was beautiful, with loads of stop-off places along the way. The weather was OK but not red hot.

On the way I saw one of the saddest things I had ever seen in my life. A mother kangaroo had been crossing the road and had been knocked down by a car. Her little baby had come out of its pouch to see what had happened and he had been killed as well. It was so sad.

On our map we found a nice place to stay in Melbourne. It was the sort of small Melbourne street you would see on Neighbours. The site had a lovely swimming pool, so we were hoping that tomorrow we would be able to sit there and chill out.

10TH MARCH

We survived the first night in our camper and were even still speaking the next morning. I quite liked the wine box, complete with its own tap. It was quite a challenge trying to make the bed up half cut and trying to be quiet. It poured with rain all night, so we found out it didn't leak. When you have no toilet though, the last thing you need is to be able to hear the rain beating on the roof. We had another twenty-seven nights in it.

We went for a walk around the area and saw lots of beautiful colourful parrots and various other birds, and it was lovely to see them flying in their natural habitat instead of in cages, which I hate. The woods were lovely and there was a gorgeous lake nearby.

11TH MARCH

It was red hot, so we spent the morning at the pool. Not a lot of people were using the pool area, so we practically had it to ourselves. Tony managed after only one day to break one of the picnic chairs. He said it was already broken. I don't know how he said that with a straight face.

We spent some of the morning at the pool, then caught the train into Melbourne town. It was a lovely journey watching out of the train windows as we passed houses and streets and scenery. When we got off the train at the old railway station, which was a beautiful building, we saw how nice the city centre is. The architecture was spectacular.

We could hear screaming and shouting and thought there was a demonstration or something going on until we turned the corner and saw a lady (and I use the word loosely) lying on the pavement howling and kicking and making it very difficult for the police who were trying to arrest her and get handcuffs on her. It's not what you would see on an episode of Neighbours, put it that way. She was cursing and lashing out with her fists and feet while a crowd had gathered around. Ah, the memories of policing!

After the 'performance' we decided to go and have a look at the art centre. We walked around and looked at some of the stuff, which in my opinion was mostly crap. I know art is about creating debate, but I don't get some of it. Surely you don't have to hang a picture consisting of a few lines and say its art to create debate. Drink with my mates and you'll find out what debates are all about. My mate Stevie could start an argument in a monastery.

12TH MARCH

We caught the 'free bus tour', which would have been great if they had not piled so many people on. All I saw for the whole journey was the back of a Led Zeppelin T Shirt (nice T shirt mind). Afterwards Tony bought us lunch in the shape of a sandwich from the local newsagent.

Surviving in the camper van without injury was a real test of wits, and you needed nerves of steel. The inside was tiny, there was nowhere to sit once the bed was made up and there was no toilet on board, so in the night when you needed the loo it was a mission in itself.

13TH MARCH

This morning we moved along the coast to another small site on the outskirts of Melbourne, where we stayed for two nights before moving on. I bought myself an extra large wine glass for use in the night, because it was cheaper than a small one, and the ones in the van were too small.

In the night I was in a deep sleep when I was woken by a loud crash and saw the bed had collapsed and Tony was wedged in the hole in the middle. The table sat on two small lips with just an extra piece of wood to take the mattress, so it was only a matter of time before it collapsed under us. It took us ages to get it sorted and eventually get back into bed, and then half an hour later it collapsed again. It was the same routine of having to pull Tony out of the hole in the middle of the bed and put the wood back in. Eventually we managed to get it sorted without it collapsing.

When we woke up the weather was lovely. It was windy, but it had blown up a brilliant surf. We watched the surfers on the beach. Some of the kids were as young as five years old and were already brilliant. We did a bit of body surfing and loved it, but we were definitely not ready for a board yet.

When we got back to the van the sky very quickly turned black and we got pelted with berries off the trees, as the wind was blowing them off. A tremendous storm blew up and lasted for about two hours. It was the kind of storm you only expect in Kansas. Within minutes the rainwater was six inches deep on the road and everyone was running for cover. The Aussies we spoke to said they were having freak weather.

We sat in the van listening to the rain on the roof, which I think is a lovely sound. I was so pleased we packed waterproof jackets. I wasn't expecting storms here - I really packed them for the jungle.

The weather was pretty bad and didn't look like it was going to give up. On the way back from the beach I found a piece of wood that I thought I could wedge under Tony's side of the bed to stop it collapsing again. If it did collapse I was afraid Tony would be pierced by the wood, like Dracula in his coffin.

15TH MARCH

The piece of wood worked, and the bed did not collapse in the night. Mind you we were both totally paranoid about moving in it. We drove along the A1 road along the coast, the coastline and countryside is beautiful.

We saw loads of kangaroos, but they were all dead. Either there were a hell of a lot of them or they were really shit at the Highway Code. We were looking forward to hitting the start of the Grand Pacific Highway that would take us right up to Sydney. We were going to stay two nights in a hostel there and enjoy being back in a real bed once again.

We stopped at a place called Eden, which was a lovely little town with an old court house and police station dating back to 1837. Both are still in operation today and some of the locals walking around town looked like they could have quite easily been born the same year as the town.

The local magistrates each had their names on a board at the door of the courthouse telling everyone their name, year of birth and occupation. They had all been born in the town, were all over sixty years old and were all ex-teachers or other various professions. You got the impression they didn't take any shit and if you were up in front of them you should be afraid, very afraid. It made us think we should have magistrates like this at home, but as a trained magistrate myself (yes it's true) I can tell you we are governed by charts and red tape.

There was a board outside the courthouse giving details of who was up in front of the magistrates today, and I would have loved to have gone in and sat in the public gallery to observe, but it was closed for lunch. Besides, Tony has a fear of courtrooms, which is probably because of the amount of time he spent in them in his youth. For doing 'nothing wrong', he says.

We sat at the harbour and watched the fishermen come to shore with their catch. They unloaded it straight to the local restaurants and hotels, where it is cooked to the customer's specification. You can't get fresher than that.

We found a gorgeous coffee shop with free Wifi, so we sat and watched the world go by and caught up with the local gossip from home. Surprisingly we were not even missing home. We had so much we wanted to see and do.

I lay awake half the night listening to the rain which was in unison with Tony's snoring. All was going well, and after several sharp punches to the kidneys he somehow wasn't snoring quite as loudly. At last I was dropping off when there was a loud crash and Tony was lying half in the bed and half in a hole where the bed had once been. He hadn't wedged the piece of wood in properly.

I tried to pull him out of the hole, which was not easy. I now wanted to drive the van back to the hire place and throw the keys at them along with the piece of wood. I couldn't, so I resigned myself to getting him out of the hole.

It reminded me of the time when I was young and went for my tea at a friend's house. I was sitting at the table and thought no one would notice if I pulled the table towards me instead of having to stand up and pull my chair closer. I gently pulled the table when no one seemed to be looking, then suddenly realised that it was opening in the middle and the chicken was slowly sliding towards the gap in the centre. It was all in slow motion to me, but it was probably moving pretty quick. Someone suddenly realised what was happening and pulled the cloth, saving the chicken from disappearing into the hole.

Anyway I was now trying with all my might to pull my seventeen-stone pissed husband out of this hole. I somehow managed it and the bed once again had to be fixed with the wood well and truly wedged into position. I lay on the side clinging on like a praying mantis for the rest of the night and Tony was ordered not to even think of moving.

We woke up with no further mishaps, but I felt as if I had been in traction for a month and my finger was broken. I was hoping it wasn't the dreaded curse that had been put on me for not buying the bracelet. In the morning Tony couldn't really remember what all the fuss was about.

16TH MARCH

Tony has now managed to break both the picnic chairs. He said they were cheap and nasty anyway. Personally I would rather sit on cheap and nasty chairs than none at all. I had to get the information pack out and telephone the camper van hire firm and explain to them that the chairs had both broken. Because it was both of them, I think they were convinced that they couldn't have been in very good condition to begin with. After all, the inspection of the van before we could drive it away had taken all of ten minutes. They were fine about it and gave me the go-ahead to buy two replacement chairs and keep the receipt to be re reimbursed, so after dinner we headed out to look for a shop that sold picnic chairs.

The great thing about the little camper was that when you wanted to go out for the day it didn't take long to pack up and drive off. There were a few places we passed that sold picnic chairs, but they were expensive and not that good quality, so we decided to look for a cheaper place. Eventually I spotted a camping accessory shop.

Tony says 'Do you think they sell chairs?'

'Probably, it's a camping accessory shop. I'd be surprised if they didn't. What do you think?'

'I'm not sure, you'll have to ask, they might not sell chairs.'

'I think they will Tony, it's a camping accessory shop.'

Eyes to the ceiling and dirty looks come my way. 'Well if they don't, then don't blame me.'

'No Tony, I won't blame you, because I will be too fucking amazed if they don't sell chairs.'

We pulled up outside the shop and I went inside the store. Ten minutes later I returned to the camper van with two new picnic chairs and Tony said

'That was a bit of luck.'

'No Tony, there was no luck was involved. It's a camping accessory shop, what did you think they were going to sell?'

'They might not have had any chairs, though.'

'Tony, SHUT THE FUCK UP.'

Now my marriage vows and my patience are being tested to the extreme.

Ladies, I can highly recommend any of the following wines -

Sovereign Point, Fruity Lexia and Walkley Vintners. After two large glasses it makes any husband tolerable, and if you happen to be on Weightwatchers and are sick you could have all your points again.

17TH MARCH

We survived another night in the camper van and I was beginning to feel like Ray Mears. The weather was not too warm and it was a nice day to walk, so we walked on the beach looking for live kangaroos. We saw what looked like a moving blanket of blue on the sand, and as we got closer we saw that it was hundreds of the most amazing blue crabs, all walking together. They were beautiful.

When we got back to the site we found that two girls had pulled up alongside us. Tony was convinced that they were the two lesbians from the hostel in Adelaide, but they didn't even look the same. Either way, we decided to leave tomorrow.

18TH MARCH

We packed up, which took all of ten minutes, and drove north along to Bateman's Bay, which is the most beautiful drive. In October and November you can stop and watch the whales leaping in the sea. We are fortunate to have seen this in North America many years ago. If you get the chance it's a fantastic sight to see, the sheer size of the whale is incredible.

On the drive we passed through places called Merimbula and Wolumia, typical Australian names. The Grand Pacific Drive encompasses some of the most spectacular coastline in New South Wales and Australia. The drive is 140km long and it takes you through coastal rain forests, little quaint villages, coastal towns, rolling hills, wineries and dairy farms. The iconic sea cliff bridge is

665 metres long and is truly beautiful, although in my opinion it is better looking up at it than when you are actually on it, as like the Golden Gate Bridge in Francisco or any other bridge for that matter, even our Tyne Bridge, you don't appreciate it when you are actually on it because of the side construction.

Bateman's Bay is on the banks of the river Clyde and the Eurobodalla nature coast and we were not disappointed - it was gorgeous. The beaches were fabulous, it was all little beach-front cafés and restaurants and there were dolphins showing off in the water right in front of us. I love their little faces - they always look like they are smiling at you.

The seafood here is supposed to be the best for miles around, and we could see fishermen catching fish and cooking it for you right there and then. The oysters are very popular here, but I didn't want to try those. I didn't fancy an aphrodisiac with a bit of wood holding the bed up.

We had to drive to the local liquor store for our supplies. I can't get used to this drinking inside lark, I'm a pub girl through and through. Or as Tony says 'You can take a girl out of Newcastle but you can't take Newcastle out of the girl'.

My tan is fading quickly and that smell is following me around. I'll find out eventually what it is.

19TH MARCH

The rain didn't stop all night. It's quite scary the way the sun can be shining one minute, then the sky is black the next.

We bought some fruit to feed the parrots later. Today we sat and watched the massive pelicans doing their own diving and fishing, flying and dropping into the sea and not missing anything, the fish didn't stand a chance. We walked for miles along the coast and had a coffee in the oldest café in Bateman's Bay, which was lovely.

CHAPTER NINE

20TH MARCH

We woke up after a horrendous storm during the night. We couldn't believe the amount of rain, it was pouring non-stop all night. It was like being in a tin can. I usually love it when it's raining like that, but it's quite frightening when it's so persistent. The bed didn't collapse, which was the high point of the evening. The shoes we left outside were completely soaked. Mine were just my plastic flip flops, but Tony had left his trainers out. It was still raining when we woke up, and we had to wait to leave the site because of a landslide a few miles along the coast road.

It was pretty scary when we saw how the rain had flooded the roads and how muddy they were, along with fallen trees and branches. After waiting around for a while we were told of the exact location of the landslide, so we headed off in the opposite direction. We arrived at a place called Depot Beach and decided to camp in an area of National Forest called Murramarang. We wanted to experience the real outdoors, despite the size of the spiders that lurk in these parts. We were being brave because I felt sure it would be worth it. There were kangaroos everywhere, and judging by the amount of kangaroo shit they were being well fed. I don't think even Scooby Doo's gardener has seen this much crap.

We parked the camper and headed off into the forest. I was hoping that nothing would crawl up my leg, because I only had cut-offs on. The forest here was spectacular. The termite hills were the size of garden sheds, so God only knows how many termites it took to build them. We saw the biggest spider of our lives. Luckily it was dead and had its legs curled up, but it was still massive. Nearby there was a web, and in it was a thing that looked like a fly but was the size of a pound coin, so if it was a fly it was a big one. There was half of what looked like a tarantula in the web, and its spidery legs were poking out. That reminded me to do my bikini line.

When we returned from the forest we walked on the beach and sat and watched the kangaroos playing with each other. They were boxing and playing together, an amazing sight. Tony wanted to box with one, but when it looked like the kangaroo was going to be up for it he backed down.

We returned to our camper and decided to cook our food. You will be pleased to hear that it didn't contain any kangaroo steaks. Next to where we were parked was an empty self-contained cabin (which I think is cheating in the forest), and I had a look inside, as it just happened to be open. Inside there just happened to be a microwave, so I nipped in while Tony kept watch and took advantage of it. (Now that IS cheating in the forest).

We were sitting at the picnic table eating and were deep in conversation when we looked at each other and realised we had guests with us. There was a kangaroo at each end of the table. What a surreal experience.

'What's that Skippy, you want more potatoes?' I said. 'Tut tut tut' was Skippy's reply, which as we all know can mean anything from 'John's stuck down the well and needs help' to 'Jessie's lying injured in the forest.' On this occasion it obviously meant 'Aye, go on then' (he was a Geordie kangaroo, naturally). Well all right, he was probably Australian.

After tea when we had retired and six-dinner Skippy had hopped off for second helpings somewhere else, I put some chopped apple out for the parrots. I'm not a great lover of birds flying around you, but I never thought there would be so many. Within minutes you couldn't see for parrots. A giant one (apparently there is always one giant one, this one was plain red in colour) decided to land in my hair. It was like a scene from The Birds, a real Tippi Hedren experience. I didn't like it in my hair, but Tony thought it was hysterical. We hand-fed them and they were gorgeous. How anyone can keep a bird in a cage is beyond me.

We sat in the van and it was absolutely pitch black, so of course we told each other ghost stories, which was a really sensible idea on a black night with the toilet block at the other end of a field. After we had scared the shit out of each other we made the bed up to sleep. In the night I woke up needing to go to the toilet, probably because I had been listening to the pouring rain, and I must confess my extra large wine glass took a bit of a hammering. I was now wishing we had not told ghost stories. It was black and I couldn't see a thing.

Something was making a very strange noise in the forest, and to say I was scared is an understatement. I took a few deep breaths and opened the door. I had already made my mind up that I was going to use the toilet in the 'great outdoors', but as I opened the door to get out a head came through. I screamed and nearly had a heart attack. Then something touched my leg. I was convinced we were going to be butchered in the forest like some backpackers I had read about travelling through Australia.

Tony woke up, and we were both screaming and shouting in total panic. By this time I had nearly wet myself anyway. I somehow managed to grab the torch and shone it to see if it was indeed Freddie Kruger, but to my relief it was just Skippy standing there. For fuck's sake Skippy! But I was so pleased to see him.

He just looked at me and said the usual 'tut tut tut', which I didn't bother trying to translate at three in the morning.

21ST MARCH

We had survived yet another exciting night, with another massive storm as well as an insomniac kangaroo. We left early after saying goodbye to Skippy and hit the road, listening to the radio and watching the weather getting worse. There was no mention of any killer kangaroos on the loose, which made me feel better. Mind you,

I think me and Skippy had bonded by the time I left.

The radio was advising us to go slow and only drive if we really needed to. We were booked into our next site, so we took our time.

We arrived at the site in Kiama after a treacherous drive and the rain was still belting down hard and fast. That's the great thing about having such a tiny van I suppose, you literally drive straight on to a site and there's nothing much to do except reach up and retrieve the wine glasses.

We had to drive down a hill on to the site. We got booked on and parked up, hoping the rain would eventually stop, or at least lay off a bit. There was no way we could go outside, so we settled down for a game of Scrabble. Needless to say the wine box and extra large wine glass came out.

We were happily sitting there when we saw a man walking towards our van. We slid the door open and found he had come to give us our shoes, which we had left at the top of the site and had now been covered by a river of rainwater. We didn't realise how deep the water had got in such short time.

We needed to move the van to higher ground while we could. We stepped out and were immediately up to our ankles. When we saw how many people were moving around, some of them waist deep, we realised this was serious. We knew we had to try and move the camper, and as we had not long arrived I could visualise where the road was, so I walked in front, making sure I was on the road, while Tony drove behind me. The water was coming in through the door, but he had to keep driving.

We managed to park on high ground at the front of the site. Just as we reached this point the creek at the bottom of the site broke its banks, and we watched helplessly as three or four camper vans went underwater. We would have been one of them - we had a miraculous escape.

We heard that some of the owners were stuck along the road due to another landslide, so they could not get to their vans. The whole site was in chaos and there were trees and debris floating past.

After a few hours the rain had still not subsided, and although we were on higher ground we were now facing the possibility of a landslide as we were parked down in a valley. We had no choice but to stay in the van as the rain was so bad. Water levels were a foot deep everywhere on the site, including the communal kitchen block.

Needless to say we had a very restless night, but we survived.

22ND MARCH

After being awake nearly all night terrified that we would be swept away, we were pretty knackered the next morning. We looked out of the window and saw that the water level had dropped significantly, but it had left loads of debris including several tree roots, a couple of wheelie bins with the contents strewn all over the site, and about fifty-odd flip flops.

By 10 am it looked as if nothing had happened. It was difficult to even imagine that there had been any rain - all very bizarre. The sun was shining and some people were just arriving to find their vans gone. They had not been able to get in last night after being caught in the landslide and storms along the coast.

One poor old gentleman had drowned when he had stepped the wrong way on the road, fallen into deep water and got washed away. We realised how lucky we had been. We moved our camper round to the beach, where we sat and watched the surfers resume their fun. The storm had kicked up the surf and the waves were huge.

We went out for a walk along the cliff tops and visited an infamous blow hole discovered in 1797. When the sea lashes in you get soaked and the noise is pretty loud, it's lovely. The walk takes in all the scenery and you can see for miles.

We came back and went to the beach with our towels and swimsuits to do our own version of body surfing. The sun-tanned, gorgeous men, with their six-packs, tight shorts and bleached blonde hair didn't intimidate me. In fact I hardly noticed them... Sorry, where was I? Oh yes, we had a good laugh trying the different moves. It's definitely not as easy as it looks. We didn't get any 'loops' in though, except the one that caught me off balance and threw my knickers on the beach, but apart from that we took things easy.

Back at the site people were still milling around trying to get their belongings sorted after the flood. Some people had lost everything they had when their caravans were washed away, while those which were not washed had been washed down the site and were under quite a lot of water, so the damage was irreparable anyway. Some people were talking about how their insurance had just run out, while others no doubt would be cashing in big time.

23RD MARCH

The next morning we woke up listening to the crash of the waves, with a clear view of the beach. We left the back door of the camper open and covered it with a mosquito net. It had been pretty safe so far. We sat and read the papers which had been delivered to the site that morning, but they were all shit and I missed my Newcastle Chronicle. As expected there were lots of pages covering the floods. It seemed we had been in one of the better places, judging by the number of injured people and lost possessions. The roads were soon up and running again and new arrivals were driving on to the site now.

There was a massive fox bat on the telephone wire next to the toilets. They are incredible creatures. They're called fox bats because they have the colour and shape a flying fox.

Because the weather had changed dramatically for the better, we drove out and visited the nearby town of Jamberoo, which was very quaint and reminded me of a scene from the film Deliverance. If I closed my eyes I could have heard Duelling Banjos. It felt a bit like a Northumbrian village, but on a less scary scale. Everyone seemed to be wearing checked shirts and dungarees, which I thought only Zippy and the cast of Seven Brides for Seven Brothers still wore.

According to the sign as you drive in, it has a population of 995 people. Signs like that always fascinate me, because I always wonder when it was last added to or changed. Do they send a telegram to a designated person in the vicinity (telegrams are probably still being used in this one-horse town) and say old Mrs Jenkins passed away, and then someone rushes out and changes the sign from 995 to 994? Then what happens when the next week Mrs Higgins produces her seventh child, and he's beautiful, which we all know is a complete lie because as I have already mentioned how ALL babies are ugly? He may look nicer when he's four and wears the first of many sets of dungarees and checked shirt!

I am struggling to understand where all these people live, as we have only passed twenty or so houses. Tony thinks we have stumbled into a swingers' town and thinks we should stay for a while, just as spectators. I was in agreement until we spotted a sheep being led into the local community centre.

We spotted a sign for a contemporary art centre. Every time I see anything to do with art I think of an episode when we bought our house. It's an old house and the last person to live there was an eccentric old man called Jim. It had been empty a year or so and was in quite a bad state and full of old stuff from photographs to furniture. Tony got very excited one day after our neighbour Mona and second cousin (it sounds like Jamberoo, but it's not) pointed out an oil painting on canvas. It was a portrait of a gentleman in uniform and was signed J. Reynolds. We straight away thought it was Joshua

Reynolds, and saw pound signs flashing. Tony told his father and everyone went into overdrive, convincing us we had stumbled on to a priceless painting.

Tony then informed me that he had phoned Sothebys in London and a valuer who was very interested in seeing the painting was coming the next day. We rang everyone and told them, and we were all dead excited. The next day arrived and a few people came to the house waiting in anticipation for the valuation, pacing up and down the kitchen.

Then we saw a very posh car pull up at the door and I let him in. He was the biggest snob I have ever met in my life. I saw him have a quick look around the hallway, which was in a state with the ceiling down and the panelling half painted and half not.

'Show me the painting' he said in a very deep, authoritative voice. I ushered him into the sitting room, where it was lying wrapped in brown paper (because of its value). I flipped over the paper and as he saw it he made a fist on his chest and a loud intake of breath. I thought 'Oh God it's worth a fortune' and said to him in total naivety 'What do you think?'

I will never forget the look of complete horror on his face as he replied 'That's been done by a very very very amateur hand' followed by a look that said 'Thanks for wasting my time on such a monstrosity, I'll see myself out' and wiped his feet on the way out the door.

Months later I found a photo of Jim. The picture was a self-portrait, and because of his eccentricity he had signed it J. Reynolds. We still laugh about it now. Our mate Jimmy said that on reflection it could have been done by Burt Reynolds, in a rehab session at the Betty Ford Clinic.

We decided to have a look inside the art centre anyway. To me contemporary art means weird artefacts that don't resemble anything to most people. We went inside and sure enough the art (and I use the term loosely) was displayed on the walls and various shelves and cabinets. 'Can I help you?' said someone. I couldn't resist replying 'Yes please, could you tell me what this actually is?' (Apart from being ridiculously expensive.) 'Yes madam, the artist here is telling the story of the struggle of oppression in Afghanistan and this section here depicts an area in Kabul' he said. Now you could have knocked me down with a feather, because how the hell she knew that by looking at two pieces of metal welded together in the shape of a V and covered in spray-painted cardboard was beyond me.

'Is there anything else madam?' she said. What I wanted to say was 'Yes, how the fuck did you work that one out?' but I restrained myself.

'We have a display on at the moment done by the local schoolchildren if you would like to take a look' she said. I looked at Tony and said we would like that very much. The walls in the area at the back were littered with the schoolkids' work and it was all shit, not one talented child among them. When I was at school I remember doing a Salvador Dali sketch for my 'O' level and it was excellent, so I was now thinking I would have pissed this competition. There was a photograph on display of the child with the winning entry, and just as I thought he was a precocious little brat smiling into the camera, with his over-proud mother (or in Duelling Banjos country it could have been his sister) who truly believed her child had talent.

'Would madam like anything else?' she said. I thought, 'yes, I would like a half gallon of petrol and a box of Swan Vestas' but it came out as 'No thank you' and we left Jamberoo.

25TH -27TH MARCH

We drove quite a few miles today and arrived at a place called Lake Windermere. We came on to the site after booking in and it was interesting to say the least. Judging by the static homes it appeared there were quite a few long-term residents here. They all seemed to have named their mobile homes. We were facing 'The Ponderosa' which for those of you who have seen the 'Westgate Road Ponderosa' I don't need to explain. For those of you who haven't, it's someone's front garden with a shed that has been transformed into the local bar. I don't think Claire Sweeney did this in a sixty-minute makeover, I think it took a lot less time than that. It was a place where 'interesting characters' sat and drank from cans.

There were a few blokes sitting in the sun outside the Ponderosa drinking from cans and having a heated debate. I wondered if they had been to the same contemporary art centre we had visited, because they had spiked all their empty cans on to what looked like a giant knitting needle stuck in the grass. I don't think it had anything to do with Afghanistan though, I think they were just pissed.

When we returned after getting some supplies, the Ponderosa had closed its doors. I wasn't sure if they had run out of drink or gone to bed.

The lake at Windermere was lovely, but in my opinion not as nice as the one in the Lake District.

We watched a local cricket match, because Tony wanted to watch a proper cricket match played on Australian soil. He kept telling me what was happening, because I don't have a clue when it comes to the rules of cricket. I'm only just getting to grips with the offside rule. It was good to see the match though, especially watching it in Australia where they are so passionate about the game. Mind you there wasn't much of a crowd, only a few old people in deck chairs and me and Tony, so the Mexican wave was out of the question.

When they were getting changed Tony said:

'I didn't notice they had a black lad playing for them.'

'How not?' I said.

'Cause he had his face mask on.'

'Cause he had his face mask on?'

'Well yes, I didn't know he was black.'

'Well he's got black arms.'

'Has he? I didn't notice.'

'Well of course he's got black arms, he's black.'

'Well I didn't notice.'

By this time it sounded as if we were a couple of racists. Sometimes I really worry about him.

27TH MARCH

We moved on again, through Windang and past Lake Illawarra and up into a place called Wollongong (the only place on the East Coast that can boast two lighthouses) to an area called Fairy Meadow. We booked on to a campsite which had a massive indoor swimming pool, so if the weather didn't improve we could at least still swim. The latest floods had caused quite a bit of damage and the weather again was awful, one minute nice sunshine and the next rain, wind and thunderstorms. The local skydiving club nearby still had people up in the air, so I suppose they have had worse.

The rain was persistent, which was not good, especially when we had been so used to gorgeous weather. I gave Tony his jacket and he said 'Where did I get this?' It's a miracle I haven't strangled him yet.

I have now turned the tap on. I know it sounds simple, but I am still fascinated that when you turn the tap on here the water circles the opposite way to home because we are in the Southern Hemisphere. Anyway someone, not mentioning any names but it's the person I haven't strangled yet, had left a spoon in the sink which shot all the water back and I was now drenched, which was all I needed.

Once I'd dried off I decided to occupy myself by making some tea, fresh salad with tomatoes, cucumber, lettuce, mixed peppers, onions, carrots, celery, and ham and hot potatoes, it was lovely. The sunshine came back out and we planned to eat alfresco, so we had everything on the table looking lovely and I brought out the bowls. Tony had not told me he had rigged up a washing line Heath Robinson style, so as I stepped out of the van with the salad bowl I was just about decapitated. The salad went one way and I went the other. There I was lying on the grass covered in salad, at which Tony thought it would be hilarious to say 'Is that your idea of a tossed salad?'

I had also pulled the line down and was lying with a huge pair of boxer shorts in my face. Several people had seen this and I'm sure they had the giggles. I was trying not to scream, because the pain in my neck was killing me, and Tony was standing with his can that he had managed to grab off the table before that also went over.

That's when the wine box and the salt and vinegar crisps came out.

28TH MARCH

I had the pleasure of seeing a huge spider in the awning today. I got a fright, because you hear so many tales about the poisonous creepy-crawlies in Australia. Anyway, then I got brave and knew I would have to move it, so I went in armed with a rolled-up newspaper and came out the winner.

We visited the Nan Tien Temple, which is the largest Buddhist temple in the Southern Hemisphere. Now I felt guilty about blatting the spider. Not much of a Buddhist, am I.

The coastline of Wollongong was absolutely beautiful. All along the coast were open-air swimming pools. Some were crudely cut into the rocks and were filled up by the sea, while others were professionally built with swimming lanes and you paid a fee to use them. Both kinds were spectacular, and well used. The weather seems irrelevant to the Aussies - come rain or shine, they swim. Tony says every day 'The Aussies are hard buggers'.

The cafés and restaurants along this stretch of the beach varied from the very expensive to pavement cafés for everyone's budget. There were some very expensive-looking apartments at some of the nicest points, all with balconies overlooking the ocean. The prices must have been wildly expensive - I couldn't even hazard a guess at a price tag.

The weather changed again from sunshine to rain, so we went for a swim in the indoor pool. The Aussies were still wearing their Speedos and knocking out a few lengths. The forecast was not looking too good, so we booked to stay longer. Thank God we had rain jackets. Tony said 'Have I got one?' But it was only 10 am and too early to open the wine.

We got our raincoats anyway and went off walking. We watched the Aussies swimming in the open air pools. They must be hard, it was cold and raining and they were still there. The rain got too heavy, so we headed back. We were back about an hour and sitting in the camper when a trailer tent pulled on to the site right next to us. The lad got out, had a quick look at how he had parked and didn't bother to straighten up. Instead he wound down the legs and then proceeded to open a can of beer. The sticker on his van said Newcastle, Hexham. Obviously Newcastle, Hexham in Australia but it still looked strange.

3RD APRIL

Today was the last day in the camper van, as we were looking forward to two nights of bliss in a hostel in Sydney. Our camper was very comfortable now that we had managed to get a piece of wood that we could wedge into a gap in order to stop the bed collapsing every time you turned over. I was looking forward to having a nice bed though, and a walk-in shower.

For our last night we moved to a small site called The Grand Pinks on Ramsgate Beach. It wasn't too far from where we had to drop the camper off, so only a short drive. It was a tiny site with the smallest pitches we had been on. We had two Dutch girls in a camper van next to us and Tony was convinced they were lesbians, so no surprises there then.

The birds here are incredible (not the women, although Tony might beg to differ) but the parakeets and other birds. I hate to say this but I actually had a cockatoo on my hand.

We drove for miles to the National Park to see a beach called Gawi, where the surfers meet in their droves. Seeing the white sand and huge waves I could understand why. We had to pay eight dollars to drive through the park, but it was well worth it.

The beach here was quite small and surrounded by green slopes. On the hillsides there were little shacks, built during the depression in the 1930s. There were no roads to the shacks, so people had to walk uphill for quite a distance with shopping and other supplies. I could imagine how hard that was in the 1930s, but well worth it because of the views and the fresh air. Some people today find it a hardship to carry their shopping from Iceland (the shop, not the country). Having built the shacks the people lived happily for many years in them. Some are still occupied today, while others are used as holiday homes.

When the Government reviewed its policies on the National Park they decided to get rid of the shacks because they had built a tourist car park and a café, so they issued the people with eviction orders and started to demolish the shacks. Understandably there was a massive outcry, and the demolition work was thwarted. The public were pleased that the council had backed down. It wasn't until years later that they found out what the catch was. The council had said the shacks could only be registered to the original owner – the person who had been living there since the thirties. When the original owner died the shack had to be demolished, so very soon there will be none left, which is a huge pity, as not only are they a fantastic piece of history but they are so beautiful. There are about twenty or thirty still here today, but there used to be many more. Eventually none will stand because of the bureaucratic red tape.

4TH APRIL

The following morning we emptied the van cupboards and gave away all the food we were no longer needing. A nice old couple behind us gladly took it off our hands. They were in their eighties and had been living in their camper for two years. He loved it and every day built another Heath Robinson shelf, but she looked as if she would gladly move into a bungalow tomorrow and not even keep in touch with him. He was very impressed with our own Heath Robinson anti-bed-collapse chunk of wood.

As we drove away we both felt a little sad, partly because we were giving our hippy camper van back and partly because we were going to be leaving Australia soon. But we were also both looking forward to a nice bed and en suite facilities.

While I was cleaning I finally found out what the smell was that had been following me around. It was the plastic flip flops I had bought. When I wore them and they got hot, they stank like vomit. I never noticed before on account of my belly being in the way.

We left the site and drove off in the direction of the nearest bin to discard the piece of wood we had kept to make the bed up. I didn't want them thinking we had broken it by wedging the wood underneath. I also threw the stinking flip flops in the bin.

Tony did his usual flapping and screaming while he drove us

towards Sydney and I navigated. When I told him to calm down he shouted 'We would still be in fucking Heathrow if it was left to you, you could give Mark Thatcher fucking lessons' which I took as my cue to button it. So with Tony stressed out and sweating, we eventually arrived at the return hire place. Once they had checked the van, we were off to our luxury hostel.

Everything was fine with the camper and off we went. I did feel a bit sorry when I saw the couple sitting waiting for it to be signed over to them. I was tempted to tell them where we had left the chunk of wood, but thought best no to because that would look as if we had broken it, and we hadn't. Tony said it was a design fault. They also looked small enough to be able to cope with the chairs.

Once again on foot, we set off with our rucksacks and found the main street. We jumped on a bus that said Sydney Central and then caught the train to the Kings Cross area. On arrival at our station we already had directions to the hostel, which we found in about ten minutes.

I spotted the hostel (which I can't name because I don't want to incriminate the guilty) and immediately was not impressed. The steps were minging and there was an iron door we had to knock on before we could get in. I didn't know whether to sit and cry on the step or throw myself into the path of the next bus. As we stood in the reception area our feet were sticking to the carpet. My hopes of a nice hot shower and a comfortable room were looking very dodgy now.

We got our key from the girl behind the desk, curious to see our room. I think she thought we wanted something else as we weren't going anywhere, but it was just that our feet were stuck to the carpet. Eventually we managed to pull them free and walk across the hallway. We were shown into a courtyard where our room was, and the room had a gap under the door a Jack Russell could have got under. The receptionist told us we had the best room in the hostel and the cleaners were two eighteen-year-old lads who were cleaning to earn money while they backpacked around Australia. Our 'cleaner' had clearly never cleaned anything in his life, and I couldn't tell if the rooms had been done or not. The bed was made, but that was all.

We were there for all of ten minutes when the manager, also about eighteen, appeared to tell us that we had been given the wrong key and we should in fact be upstairs. I looked up and thanked the Lord, turned quickly and headed to the staircase. On opening the door I saw that the carpet had not been vacuumed, the toilet had a nice little blob left on the side of the pan, and it was nice of them to have left the soap in the shower because once we had picked all the pubic hairs out of it we could re-use it. We had booked for two nights and had already paid on our card, so if we left we would have to pay anyway. Believe it or not, we had paid about eighty quid for this.

We decided to clean it ourselves, as the thought of them having access to our room if we complained was not a happy one. And as Tony pointed out, we were getting a free breakfast and the room had a fridge. There was also a free 'sausage and bun night' tonight, whatever that meant.

We cleaned up where we could and then ventured out. Surprisingly, a ten-minute walk away, we found the famous opera house and the Sydney Harbour Bridge. The area here was magnificent, and so opulent it was hard to believe there could be such a dive just up the street.

We passed an open-air swimming pool right on the harbour area, which was lovely. Then we walked through a beautiful park area, and there must have been about four hundred people out jogging. They really are keep-fit fanatics.

We walked around through the park, where people were sitting having their picnics, and went to see the opera house. We watched some people doing the walk over the top of the bridge. It was windy and looked a bit scary, but not as scary as the price you had to pay to do it. It was lovely to stand and look at it, because it reminded us of the Tyne Bridge. A man from Middlesbrough designed both the bridges, so it was nice to see a bit of North East Engineering admired by millions of people. I love the Tyne Bridge - when I see it I know I'm home.

We went to see Circular Quay, where the ships sailed to Gallipoli and the Dardanelles during the First World War. Most of the soldiers didn't come back, and those that did were never the same again.

It wasn't long before it was time to head back to our hovel, sorry hostel, for the free sausage and bun night. Unfortunately the hope of a hot shower was dashed as soon as I saw the state of it, but we got ready anyway and headed downstairs to join in the fun.

Almost immediately we heard someone say 'Hi you guys' and looked around to see a young girl coming towards us with her hand outstretched. It was as if she had been waiting for us to appear. 'I'm Sophia, nice to meet you both' she said. We said hello and shook hands before telling them our names. Then another voice said 'Hi, my name is Pedro', and again we had the introduction bit.

After a bit of small talk, when we asked where the bar was (there wasn't one), Tony left to go and get the cans from our room fridge. Ten minutes later and the free sausages came around on plates with the bread buns, gorgeous with all the trimmings and as much as we could eat. We were at this point wondering what the catch was, but given that it was the biggest shithole we had stayed in so far, we figured that the free sausage and bun night might just be free after all - we deserved it.

Just as we were tucking in, Pedro invited us to a 'gathering' tomorrow night organised by the church. So this was the catch. I spluttered and laughed at how naïve we had been. Tony said 'Nar Thanks' and took another bun. I was still totally pissed off with the room and the price we were paying, so one more mention of the 'gathering' and I was ready to punch Sophia anyway.

Pedro then asked me if I believed in the Lord, who I thought my God was and what he had ever done for me. I said to him that I had once prayed to God 'If you can't make me thin make all my friends fat' and he had. I was taking the piss actually, but I think he believed me, and what's worse he then thought I was a believer. After some awkward silences they soon got the message that we were not about to be converted and swiftly removed the sausages away from us to move on to the next suckers. We decided to leave, not without thanking God for the food, especially the buns, which were very fresh.

5TH APRIL

We drank enough beer last night to open a small bar, just to make us sleep. The room was still minging when I woke up even though we had cleaned it, but not as minging as the 'communal kitchen', as we were about to find out. Breakfast was in the original room in the courtyard. We found the kitchen, where we were hoping we would be able to cook something, or at least make toast. On the bench was a catering-size tub of margarine with at least twenty knives stuck in it covered in jam, marmalade and Marmite. Next to the margarine was a catering tin of jam with another twenty or so knives stuck in it, and the kitchen sink you could barely see for dirty dishes and black scrapings of burnt toast. It had burnt and caked-on food which looked like it had been on for months.

A young girl was making some toast. She buttered it and then put some jam on it, then stuck her knife back in the butter, then sat down and closed her eyes and started to pray. I think she was probably praying that it wouldn't kill her. We left and went out for breakfast and picked up a cheese pasty for the journey the next day, saving us the trouble of being financially raped in the airport.

6TH APRIL

We left the hovel at 5.45 am to catch the shuttle to the airport. We couldn't wait to get out of there, so the early bus was a bonus. We arrived at the airport at 6.30 am for our flight at 9.10 am. We found the board but couldn't see our flight, so we went over to the desk, where we spoke to a lady who told us that the desk was closed as the flight was leaving at 7.15 am.

We were in panic mode now. I was wishing I hadn't taken the piss out of God, and found myself apologising to him. While smiling and being as nice as possible, we showed her the paperwork that said our flight was departing at 9.10 am. She told us to wait, and after she had made a few phone calls she told us to go straight through and that we were expected at the other end. We were like those people you see running frantically to catch their flight and think 'why do people leave it so late?' Anyway, we made it with minutes to spare. We had no time to look round and no free spray of perfume in the duty free shop.

After a big sigh of relief we boarded the flight to Christchurch, New Zealand, and were pleasantly surprised that the flight was only two hours and twenty minutes instead of four or five hours as we'd expected. We settled down to watch out of the window and ate the cheese pasty we'd bought for the journey.

Chapter Ten

NEW ZEALAND

We had a comfortable flight to Christchurch and landed after what seemed like no time at all. Now we had to join the queue for the rigorous visa entry procedures. As we had ticked the 'nothing to declare' box confirming that we were not carrying any prohibited foodstuffs, we joined the line of waiting passengers. I was fascinated watching the dogs being led in to sniff out contraband.

Along with everyone else we were asked to put our hand luggage on the floor and step back. I love this part and was looking around for anyone that was going to get busted, as I had watched this on many occasions on the television. The dog was walked up and down the line, having a good sniff, and was being rewarded for being a 'good boy'. The line of passengers were all watching.

The dog suddenly stopped at my bag, grabbed it by the strap and started sniffing frantically. 'What's in the bag?' a very authoritative-looking woman asked. I looked on in total shock. I froze with horror and said 'nothing', shaking my head to protest my innocence. I was now being frowned at by the people in line, some were even shaking their heads. I felt like an international drug smuggler and I could see people elbowing each other. I was sweating and panicking, which made me look guilty. I was wondering if people thought I had swallowed condoms full of cocaine.

The dog continued to sniff the bag, and I was ordered to open it and show the dog. I was terrified that someone had put something in my rucksack, and was already having visions of being some big lesbian's bitch in prison. I opened the bag and the dog went mental, grabbing the strap and pulling the contents out on to the floor.

It was at that point that I saw the empty cheese pasty wrapper that Tony had obviously put in my bag. I was relieved, but I wanted to strangle him as I was led away by the lady for a lecture about not bringing food into the country, especially dairy products.

After what seemed like an eternity I was allowed out of customs, to find Tony waiting at the carrousel where we were now to collect our luggage. He was laughing and finding the whole thing a joke. After a few words, which included me telling him what a tit he was, I got my bag and headed out again through the 'nothing to declare' channel. We had already signed the declaration confirming that we had only coffee and tea in our bags, and a quick tick on the sheet as your bags go through x-ray usually enables passengers to go straight through - or so I thought.

As I went to get my rucksack off the belt I heard a familiar cry again - 'What's in the bag?' I was just about to say 'coffee and tea' when I heard 'What's this?' The customs man was pointing at a small round circle that he informed me was most probably a tin. As I struggled to get the key out of my bag to open it up for him, I noticed that some of the people who had witnessed the first episode were now watching me again. This time I really did look guilty. I was genuinely shocked, because I honestly couldn't tell you what was in the bag.

This time a very authoritative man was reminding me that when I had boarded the plane I had answered the following questions: 'Could anyone have put anything in your bag?' 'No' I had answered. 'Have you left your bag unattended at any time?' 'No.' 'Has anyone asked you to carry anything through for them?' 'No.' 'Well, I suggest you open it for me' he said. As I fumbled around looking for the key and sweating, I eventually found it and opened my rucksack. There on the top was a tin of Irish stew that I had no idea had been in there.

I could remember when we gave our food away before we handed the camper van back that Tony had wanted to take the stew. I had told him to leave it, but he had obviously hidden it in my bag. So I now had to explain why I hadn't declared it, and it wasn't even mine. But I could hardly say 'Well actually my husband has interfered with my luggage and put it in my bag'. I had to look sorry as I was reprimanded and reminded in no uncertain terms to declare all goods in future. I was then reminded that I could have been looking at a hefty fine. I looked over and saw Tony shaking his head as if to say 'I told her', and at that point I swear I was that far away from bashing his brains out with the tin of Irish stew.

Eventually we were allowed outside the airport, still being looked at as if we had something to hide. I can hear them now saying 'It's always the ones you don't suspect'.

We caught the shuttle bus to the hire place to pick up our next camper van, which I'm glad to say was a lot bigger than the one we'd had in Australia. Because of the recent earthquake we decided to spend the first night not too far from the centre to make our plans, because some places were now no-go areas. It's just as well we did, because the gas bottle and the sink were both leaking. We were either going to drown or get gassed to death. Given the way things had gone since we'd landed in New Zealand, it was looking likely that something would go wrong. I thought of all the disasters we had missed, and I was now going to be serving a life sentence for smuggling a cheese pasty wrapper and a tin of Irish stew into the country. Either that or for murdering Tony with the stew.

CHAPTER TEN

7TH APRIL 2011

We soon found that it was impossible to get anywhere near the city centre. The army had it cordoned off, along with many of the roads, and there were posters up everywhere advertising for information about missing people who might have been involved in the earthquake. Everywhere we went we met people who had lost their homes, their belongings, or worse, a family member or friend. It was terribly sad.

We realised then that the information we had been getting at home about the quake had been minimal, and the devastation was on a much more massive scale. You could feel the desperation of people and the sadness of loss. The feeling of not being able to help or do anything for them was dreadful.

We found a route and drove the van back to exchange it for a new one. The temperature here was now seven degrees and it was bloody freezing, but thankfully we found a few second-hand shops and kitted ourselves out for the cold. I even found a fan heater for five bucks. The heater might just push Tony over the edge. I have to say the edge, as it would be impossible to drive him to drink.

When we were all sorted with the new camper, we took off and drove over New Zealand's longest bridge. It was lovely, on one side we saw snow-covered mountains and on the other there were vineyards.

We came across a gorgeous little place called Geraldine, which was a real little picture-postcard town, although it was also quite surreal because it looked as if it belonged to a scene from *Little House On The Prairie*. It was a bit like Jambaroo only the people here didn't look as inbred. The town consisted of a cinema, which was donkeys' years old and was protected (probably by John Boy and Laura), a school (where Laura was probably a teacher), a local food store, a few shops and a residents' club. In the supermarket there were a load of women crowding around looking at the wall, so I decided to take a look. It was an Easter egg painting competition, all done by five to twelve year olds, and needless to say they were all shit. I mean, asking me for my opinion on something like that is like asking Emu not to peck you. It's game on.

We parked the van on a site called the Geraldine Kiwi and decided to check out the local club to see how much the beer was and to give ourselves a treat. There was a bloke in the bar who was so bent over he could have been kissing his belly button. He'd either spent too much time in a hippy camper van or he had serious spondylosis.

We asked what time it closed and the barman told us it was when the last person left. We treated ourselves to a beer. It was us who were the last out the door. At 8.45 pm.

We walked back to the site and it was totally pitch black, not a light on in any of the houses. It was as if everyone had just disappeared without warning, there was literally no sign of life anywhere. It was all very strange.

10TH APRIL

Drove along Highway One to Dunedin, which is based on Edinburgh. Very strange, because you expect to hear Scots accents. History plays a massive part in the personality of the South Island. Scottish settlers founded Dunedin and visitors can see a statue of Robert Burns in the town. They even have tatties and neeps, but as I said, no Jock accents. There's a Cadbury's factory here, so it was a knocking bet that that was going to be getting a visit. We booked on to the Dunedin Kiwi site, which we found on the internet.

It had got a bit chilly now to surf and swim, which was a shame because the site was right across from the beach. Instead we went off in search of the penguins that apparently come to the beach every night at five o clock. Not sure how they knew what time it was, but that was the story.

It got to five o' clock and not a penguin in sight, but we spotted a huge thing on the beach that we initially thought was a rock and turned out to be an elephant seal (at least we think it was an elephant seal). We wouldn't have spotted it if it hadn't moved. Being brave, we climbed down the cliff edge on to the sand for a closer look. It was massive. I now know why the little penguins hadn't come out. We took some pictures of it and remembered not to stand in its path, as apparently they can shift when they need to. Who said fat lasses couldn't shift?

We left the seal and went in search of the penguins, but we were disappointed. After a while we decided they weren't going to come out, so we headed back to the luxury of our camper van. We got the usual bag of pasta and onions and headed off to the communal kitchen to cook. After our tea, when the heater had been on for five minutes, one of the first of many fights started.

'I'm boiling' said Tony.

'Ahhh for Christ's sake man, it's frigging freezing!'

'Well, I'm hot.'

'Well it's staying on for a bit, 'cause my hands are purple'

'I bet me face is red.'

'It's not.'

'Well what colour is it then?'

'The usual, purple.'

'Ha ha, very funny.'

'I wasn't trying to be.'

Get me back to the warm weather, will you.

11TH APRIL

Up early, dead excited about going to the Cadbury's factory, thinking Willy Wonka and gobstoppers. 'La la la la la I've got a golden ticket' I sang as we showered and shaved – well, Tony shaved, I didn't need to. I was concentrating on being quiet after sneaking into the gents' shower room because of the queue at the ladies. Sod that, I thought when I saw it, I've got a factory to visit.

Off we went on the local bus, which was driven by a lad from Carlisle. Tony only said to the lad 'Two to the Cadbury's factory' and he replied 'a see ya team got beat yesterday'. We had a bit of crack with him and he said he drove buses in Carlisle. I said 'So did you get lost, 'cause you're a long way from Carlisle?' He said 'Oh no, I came here to live and now I work on the buses here'. I think he thought I was serious.

Anyway we arrived at the factory, which was all purple like you'd expect, and I was dead excited to go in. Tony was pretending he wasn't, but I think he was. Once inside we were put into groups of ten, and then as we got to the entrance we were instructed by a woman resembling Kathy Bates to remove all our jewellery and cover our hair with the hairnets provided. I had lots of beaded bangles on my wrist which I had bought in Thailand, so I hid them under my sleeve.

I had already told Tony not to accept any sweets off anyone resembling an oompa loompa, and judging by Kathy Bates the thought of meeting an oompa loompa was frighteningly real. We were escorted into an area where apparently some of the sweets were made, but there was no one around and the machine was standing idle. We then had to answer questions for prizes, which were of course sweets. We were being treated like schoolchildren, though there wasn't anyone under the age of 30 in our group. If you shouted out the answer before you put your hand up, you didn't get the sweet.

Along another corridor and more questions, to which surprisingly most of us had started putting our hands up. She said to the group 'Name five Cadbury's products'. Tony shot his hand up with great pride, saying 'Me me me' under his breath. He was so chuffed when she pointed at him and this bloke next to us said to his wife 'I had my hand up first' at which his wife promptly nudged him in the ribs. Tony, with a huge grin on his face, said 'Smarties'. He was just about frogmarched out there and then. 'No no no!' said a horrified looking Kathy, shaking her finger at him. She asked the next person with their hand up, who was the same bloke who had said to his wife that he'd had his hand up first. He glanced at Tony with a smug look on his face before reeling off five Cadbury's products.

I knew then that war had commenced. 'Bastard' said Tony under his breath as Kathy threw a Mini Twirl out. We had only been there for ten minutes and already we were turning into kids.

I heard Kathy Bates shout 'What's that on your wrist?' and just about died on the spot, only to spin round and see her talking to a young girl who had the same beaded bangles on as I did. She gave her a lecture about how the whole factory would have to close if only one bead was missing. Considering that we had seen everything through wire mesh and nothing had been operating, I think Kathy was over-reacting a bit, but just the same I hid mine back under my sleeve.

The tour wasn't that good, in fact a huge disappointment if I'm honest. We didn't see much in the way of production. We did see a ton of chocolate being dropped out of a huge chute, but the rest of the factory was behind wired barriers. People were excited at seeing so much chocolate, but I was thinking I had dipped more in my coffee on my biscuits. I'm not even sure there was anyone working there, because we only saw a few people in white overalls and white wellies going for lunch. We did get some freebies, but not what we expected, it was cheap marshmallow covered in chocolate. Not good enough -

I wanted a family-size bar of Fruit and Nut at least, but we did get a voucher for discount in the shop afterwards. We bought some chocolate anyway.

When we got back to the van I had been expecting to be full of chocolate, so I was in a total strop. The nice thing was that we had some resident ducks on the site. I made the mistake of throwing bread at them and we were now being mobbed. They were actually coming into the van, which I thought was taking the piss a bit, and Tony was going mad because they were shitting everywhere. I liked them though.

That night we went in search of the penguins again. Still not one in sight, but we did see an albatross, which was fantastic and bloody massive. Tony said 'She can stick her fucking Twirl up her arse, this is much better' (but he wasn't bitter, honest).

Disappointed again, we walked back to the camper van in readiness for another fight about the fan heater. We had seen an albatross - how much better could it get? We were on a lovely pitch, and then a van with four Chinese on board pulled up next to us. We'd thought we were going to be on our own. Never mind.

12TH APRIL

Now I'm not accusing the Chinese people of anything, but there was a distinct lack of ducks this morning and no matter how much bread I threw out they didn't come. That's all I'm saying.

We packed up and decided to head to Invercargill. It was quite strange seeing all the Scottish names. We drove about fifty miles in the wrong direction and of course it was my fault. I reminded Tony that he was the one holding the steering wheel and he said 'Just as well', and I finished it with 'We would still be in Heathrow if it was left up to you'. He wouldn't let it go. I still didn't get how it was my fault. I said 'If you're in a taxi and the driver takes you to the wrong place then it's his fault, he's driving. Surely it's your fault?' Tony said 'No its not, and stop calling me Shirley'.

We played with the idea of carrying on in the same direction, but we changed our mind and turned round. We were glad we did had as we got to stop off at a place called Nugget Point, where we sat and watched baby seals playing. We managed to get quite close, which was an added bonus. It was gorgeous to watch them in the wild instead of in a zoo. We stayed there for quite a while, then headed on through Montrose and into the National Park, where we stayed at a site called Beach Road. There were lots of different animals here running free and loads of birds, which pleased Tony, who had now turned into Victor Meldrew. 'Great, more frigging bird shit' he said.

13TH APRIL

Tony was very excited when I suggested a day in the bush. First he said 'Where did I get this jacket?' then after I'd hit him we went walking. We saw loads of gorgeous birds. There were quite a few we didn't recognise, but we did see fantails and tuis. We only knew what a tui was because it was on the front of a beer bottle, the beer being called after the bird.

There were static homes behind the site where some people lived all year round. A tiny kitten wandered into our van, and its owner appeared some time later looking for it and took it home. The site was lovely. As we sat outside we watched a squirrel up a tree and the site owner came and was pointing the different birds out to us.

We went to make dinner in the communal kitchen, and while our pan was boiling we watched a tiny mouse come out from under the cupboard and drag away a piece of potato. It reminded me of the mouse in the film The Green Mile.

I was sitting minding my own business when a huge moth flew in. I hate them so I flew out, which a lady nearby thought was really funny. Tony got the moth out and I went back in. About half an hour later I took great delight when the little mouse ran over the kitchen floor and the same woman that had laughed at me screamed and ran out. Good old Stuart.

14TH APRIL

We moved on to Queenstown today, and it was a lovely place. Nestling on the shores of Lake Wakatipu, it's surrounded by the Southern Alps. Apparently early settlers believed it was good enough for Queen Victoria, hence the name Queenstown, so if it's good enough for Her Majesty it's good enough for me and big H.

We pulled on to a camp site and a cable car sat right above us. The views from the top were beautiful, we could see for miles. The site was nice but very cramped, probably because this is a very touristy area and we had been used to smaller sites in the forest. Compared to the other sites this one was quite expensive, and you had to pay two dollars for an eight-minute shower. Tony said he wasn't getting a shower on principle, and I thought, we'll see.

While we were in the kitchen we met two older travellers from Canada who were cycling around South Island. We were quite impressed until after speaking to them for five minutes we realised that they were patronising twats and so far up their own arses they could probably see their Adam's apples. We struck them off our list of people to speak to.

We went for a walk around the lake, which was lovely. The parks here are littered with little barbecue areas and bench seats. We spotted the van we had taken back because of the leaking gas and sink. We saw a couple getting into it, and I was tempted to ask for my bag of pegs back. Tony wasn't convinced it was ours, but it was, they all have names and this one was Jaffa.

We sat doing our favourite thing, people watching. After a while we decided on booking a trip to Milford Sound, which is one of the unofficial wonders of the world.

15TH APRIL

Sent Tony off with his two dollars and his wash bag. Principle my arse! We walked down into the local village, which was just five minutes away, and boarded our luxury coach complete with television and air con to go to Milford Sound. It was the business. On the bus a couple next to us had their packed lunch, a small sandwich each, an apple and a bag of carrots. They looked like a couple of tree-huggers who go to parties and make dream catchers and fry placentas while reading the lentil-eaters' manifesto. We had four sandwiches each and a steak pie. We spotted the arsehole cyclists on the coach and decided not to speak.

The driver gave us the safety advice, which was boring and long-winded. I was hoping it would be more like what Mrs Brown would say: 'Ladies and gentlemen, In the unlikely event of a fire I would like to tell you what steps to take.' Pause. 'Fucking big ones.'

That wasn't all. 'Ladies, if you need to break the windows you can do this by tapping the corner of the glass with the heel of your shoe' he said. Now hold on a minute, no one told me you had to have shoes with heels, I only had tree-huggers' sandals. I realised that along with my packed lunch I had a bar of thick toffee which I was sure would do the job. Having said that, if we didn't crash in the next ten minutes I would have eaten it. Bollocks, I trusted the driver. I was eating my toffee.

I looked over and saw the bag of carrots had come out. Not much of a match for toffee. For eating or for breaking windows.

The views through the windows of the coach got better and better. The scenery through the alpine trees and mountains was breathtaking, like the Norwegian fjords. When the coach stopped for people to take photographs, you could smell the pine.

After a few stops we got to the boat, which I'm pleased to say had a lovely inside area where you could get coffee and snacks. Off we sailed up the fjords, and it was gorgeous. The boat stopped at a waterfall called Sterling, where legend has it that if you stand under the spray for more than ten seconds you wake up looking ten years younger. A few women practically shoulder-charged everyone out of the way just in case it worked. No one left it to chance, so we stood there anyway.

A pod of about twenty dolphins swam alongside our boat (probably saying to each other 'look at these idiots under the spray'). The water was crystal clear, so you could see every one of them. They had gorgeous little faces. I was so glad I only eat dolphin-friendly tuna.

We stopped the boat many times to see the scenery, which was breathtaking. The sculptural shapes of the mountains send natural waterfalls cascading down below. It reminded us very much of Halong Bay in Vietnam, which is another 'unofficial' wonder of the world.

At the beginning of the journey it was pouring of rain and we were worried it was going to spoil the trip, but then the sun started shining. The dolphins followed the boat on several occasions and we passed many waterfalls.

We got back and decided to stay out for a few beers because we had found a bar that was not too expensive and sold beer by the jug. We wished it had been Vietnamese or Cambodian prices though. It was run by a young woman who originated from the UK and still had family living in Heaton, Newcastle upon Tyne - small world. Tony thought she was canny, but I thought she was a pain in the arse. I might have changed my mind if she had given us a beer on the house, but she didn't, so she was a pain in the arse.

After a few large jugs of beer we walked back to the van, where another fight ensued because of the fan heater.

16TH APRIL

Well I definitely didn't look ten years younger this morning. In fact I felt ten years older, probably because of the beer last night. Tony's face was red and had a healthy glow, but I think that was because of the fan heater, not the waterfall. I thought he was actually going to murder me last night and all over the bloody fan heater, but I lived to tell the tale.

17TH APRIL

Drove to Fox Glacier, which was beautiful. We passed the two people who were cycling and didn't feel any pity for them as we passed. The rain was beating down on the windscreen while we sat in the comfort of our van.

We got further along the road and I was struggling in second gear as we passed a group of about ten cyclists all wearing 'Wanaka Cycling Team' shirts (Wanaka being the next village along). The route they were riding was completely incredible, up and over the mountains. The gradient was unbelievable, and they made it look easy. Can't have been a total bunch of Wanakas.

We arrived at a site we were going to stay on, and as we booked in Tony said to the lady behind the desk 'Are there any barbers or hairdressers nearby?' She looked at Tony with her eyelashes fluttering and reached out to ruffle his hair. 'Oh, you don't need much done, you look fine to me' she said. Tony said 'It's for her' and pointed at me. She then put on her glasses and looked over the top of them at me and said 'Oh yes, right. No there aren't'.

After Tony's flirting was over we got the van set up on the site and went out for a walk. We bought a newspaper at a small shop on the way, because there had been another earthquake in Christchurch and we wanted to read about the areas that it had affected.

The walk was beautiful and very peaceful. There wasn't anyone around apart from the odd car that drove past us. We stumbled across the local cemetery and had a look around. It was ancient and beautifully kept. The weather was cold but nice and fresh. We thought we could hear an owl in the distance, until we passed a bloke carrying his kid, who was having a screaming temper tantrum. The thought of smacking it with the rolled-up newspaper crossed my mind, but I thought I'd better not.

We went to see a lake called Mirror Lake, which was beautiful. We then reached the glacier, which was something spectacular. We didn't walk up to the top of the glacier, only the bottom - you have to go with a guide if you want to climb it because you need to know where to walk and where to avoid, plus you need to have specialist clothing. We had only kitted ourselves out at the second-hand shop, so we were hardly wearing glacier thermals. The next time I eat a Fox's Glacier Mint I will think, I've walked on that glacier.

The mountains in this area are spectacular and the rock and the glacier are two million years old, or as kids would say 'as old as me nanna'. After we had taken in all the scenery we walked back to the site. When we got back Tony wanted the heater on because he was cold.

18TH APRIL

Today we drove to the Franz Josef Glacier, which was also pretty stunning. They are only 12 miles apart, so most people visit them both. I personally liked the Fox Glacier better.

We passed a young lad hitch-hiking, and he had more stuff hanging on his back than a mule could carry - pots, pans, sleeping bag, the obligatory sandals all backpackers have, although I'm pleased to say I didn't have any spare sandals. I pulled over and gave him a lift. He wanted to be dropped off in the glacier car park, where he was going to spend the night camping in the bush. By the smell of him I think he had camped in the bush before, and it could have been any kind of bush!

We sent him on his way with a couple of cans of beer and a packet of biscuits. He told us he would have to hide in the bush, as it's illegal to camp in the glacier area, and he went off like Scott of the Antarctic. The temperature drops so much at night here that I take my hat off to anyone who can sleep outdoors, not to mention the wildlife that will be lurking.

When we got back it was very cold and I couldn't help but think of him, especially as I had the fan heater going full blast.

19TH APRIL

We moved this morning to a place called Hokitika and stayed at the Beachside Holiday Park. The weather was cold, so we were very happy to discover that the site had an indoor hot tub that you could book. There were not many people on the site. We met a man originally from Nottingham who had been living on the site in his camper for the past seven years. He mined for gold in the nearby hills, and said it would pay for his flight home to the UK. During the Gold Rush in the 1860s the West Coast was one of the richest and busiest, with many people making quite a healthy profit.

There was a 'Glow Worm Den' just a ten-minute walk away, so off we went armed with our torch and winter woollies. As we approached the den area someone shouted 'Have you come to see the den?' 'Yes' we replied. So along with a few others we proceeded to follow the guide. We were led off into the pitch blackness and up a steep bank, where we were told to kick any fallen tree branches out of the way. I spotted a hedgehog in the light of my torch and was told by the guide not to touch it under any circumstances and to stop shining the light on it.

When we reached the top of the hill we could see a building that looked like a school activity centre. There were lights on which illuminated the area a bit and we could now see each other. The guide made a sweeping motion with his arm to stop anyone in his path, and shouted 'get back!' He then bent down and rubbed the bark of a fallen branch. We were all wondering what he was doing. He smelt his hand and informed us 'Yes it's a fallen branch, a victim of the recent strong winds'.

Alarm bells starting ringing, and I was wondering where this lunatic was taking us next. The other people, of which there were about five, then started to think the same, and one person started making his way back the way we had come. Everyone else started following and the guide shouting 'wait!', but we carried on making our quick exit. We just carried on, and he followed behind. At the bottom we met a few other people who were looking for the den, and among them was a local lady who had brought her grandchildren. 'Derek' she said, 'have you been telling these people you are the guide?' To which Derek replied 'No, they just followed me'. To be fair to Derek, at no point had he said he was the guide, but he hadn't said he wasn't either.

We then found out that no one is supposed to walk up to the school building – it's restricted property and the glow worm den was actually right where we had gone in. We had walked past it, but hadn't noticed because it hadn't been dark enough. The lady showed us the den, which was beautiful. It was like a million tiny fairy lights.

20TH APRIL 2011

Newcastle 0, Man Utd 0
We decided to give the 'Sock Museum' (I kid you not) a miss.

After the 'biggest toy museum in Penang' we thought better of it. We did think about visiting the Kiwi Centre to see the kiwis, but after discovering it was only one little kiwi in a cage we didn't bother. You don't see them in the wild now, or you're exceptionally lucky if you do, but I would still rather take my chances.

We booked the hot tub last night so it was ready for us, then took a bottle of wine and sat in the hot water for ages. It was gorgeous, nice and hot, and I could have stayed in there all night.

In the evening we walked to the beach to watch the sunset - I have now seen more sunsets than you can shake a stick at. To tell you the truth it couldn't disappear quickly enough for me, because it was bloody freezing. I would have given anything to be back in the hot tub. I had warned Tony that as soon as we got back the heater was going on and he agreed, I think to keep me happy.

21ST APRIL

The Hokitika Gorge was not too far away, so we went there today. It was the most beautiful blue and looked just like fabric conditioner. We crossed over the river by means of a huge rope bridge, which was scary, especially when Tony started to jump on it and make it swing from side to side. He was behaving like Indiana Jones.

We had to be careful where we ate our picnic as there was lots of wildlife and we saw signs up warning that there was a possibility of attracting unwelcome visitors. We weren't sure what kind of visitors, so we didn't open our picnic until we got back to the van.

On the drive back the sun had gone down and we passed Derek at the glow worm den waiting anxiously for new arrivals. We laughed as we watched a few people approaching and thought of him shouting 'Are you here to see the glow worm den?' and then leading everyone up the hill.

Back at the site, another camper had pulled up alongside us. It was parked far too close to the trees, but just as I was wondering how he was going to get out I saw the trees move and a man appeared, looking a bit dishevelled to say the least. He had bits of tree bark stuck in his jumper. It would have been a lot easier to have driven in again and given himself a bit more room. Later on we heard him asking where the glow worm den was and thought should we tell him about Derek, but decided it would be better if he found out himself. He looked as if he would probably get on quite well with Derek anyway.

22ND APRIL

Cape Foul Wind (and believe me it's not called that for nothing) was the destination today, along with Punakaiki, where we watched seals playing in the water, gorgeous and really close up. I can't believe I have been so close to nature in the wild. After a while we pulled over on the roadside to make coffee and a sandwich, only to discover that we had left our pans and cutlery at the site, and were over an hour's drive away. After cursing and swearing at each other and Tony reminding me again that we would still be in fucking Heathrow if it was left up to me, we decided that the best thing to do would be to buy some at the next second-hand shop.

Half an hour later we drove through a small town and spotted a second-hand shop, where we bought two knives and forks. Half way there - now we only needed two pans.

23RD APRIL

It poured with rain all night, which is great when you're in a small camper van drinking with the rain beating down, until you realise your bladder is reaching the three-gallon mark and you have to go. The water was now up to my ankles, OK for ducks but not for me. Bollocks.

We treated ourselves and went to the pub. By the time we got there I was wet through and wanted to be sat at the fire with a pint, but in New Zealand ordering a drink is a frigging nightmare. A jug is two and a half pints, a pot is just less than a pint, a 12th is a half pint and a 7th is a quarter. I was now saying through gritted teeth 'For fuck's sake man, what's wrong with a fucking pint?' Now I am no mathematician, but I did work out that the jug was better value, so we stood at the bar waiting to be served and the whole bar just about fell about laughing when Tony asked the barmaid if she had big jugs. From where I was standing I was pleased she didn't whip them out to show us, because the answer was a definite yes.

Needless to say we had a good time in the pub, which I can only describe as possibly one of New Zealand's more 'interesting'. It was even called the Black and White.

24TH APRIL

We had to drive to Picton today in preparation for the ferry crossing to North Island. We passed New Zealand's longest rope bridge, which was incredible, but because of the heavy rain we didn't get to go on it. I would have been quite scared, so I was quite pleased the weather was poor. I was now feeling fed up with the weather and wanted to get back into the sunshine, but Tony wasn't bothered.

We got the football results on the internet - Blackpool 1 Newcastle 1. Tony was happy. I have a little soft spot for Blackpool and all my friends there (you know who you are), so I wasn't too bothered that it was a draw.

We found a small site not far from the ferry terminal and decided to book on. There was a television room, which was lovely and warm, and a lovely hot shower block. The site was friendly and there were only half a dozen people on. The weather had whipped up quite a storm and we were pleased we had parked under a big tree, as we were better sheltered than others. We met a man who was also staying on the site who was part of a folk group, so he gave us a few songs and we cracked open the beers. After ages and ages we decided to get some sleep for the journey the next day.

25TH APRIL

We woke up this morning to the news that a small tornado had hit Picton in the early hours. We had slept right through it and not heard a thing. As we helped to clean up the debris we realised we had escaped yet another disaster. The roads were closed in one direction and there was a caravan blown over. It seemed we had been sheltered because we had parked under the tree.

The wind was still blowing like mad, which stopped us from doing the cliff-top walk, though Tony did say that if I wanted to go he was right behind me. After the pasty and Irish stew incident I thought better of it.

Today was ANZAC day, and it was extremely moving and very sad to see all the names on plaques and wreaths lying in the rain. Lots of older gentlemen were wearing their medals with great pride as they looked at the names, and I wondered how many of their friends were on the list. We watched the procession go by and you could see the pain still etched on their faces to this day. The sad truth is that many young people don't even know what they are marching for.

26TH APRIL

The weather was still pretty bad, and I wondered if we would be allowed to sail. I met a lady who told me she had just got off the ferry and was still green, so I was hoping against all odds that it would be cancelled. Tony told me that because the ferry was so big we wouldn't feel any movement.

We still had to make our way to the ferry, whether it was going or not, as at this point we didn't know. We drove down with extreme caution and saw the waves from the sea lashing on to the road - it looked horrendous. We joined the queue of waiting passengers, who were as much in the dark as we were, but we could see ahead of the line that there were cars driving on.

We got to the end of the line and were instructed to drive aboard. I was not looking forward to this. Once on board it felt OK, but the boat was still moving a lot.

The bar was open, so we made ourselves comfortable. I thought that if I got a seat I would probably be all right. After what seemed like ages (I was still hoping they would tell us to get off and come back tomorrow), we set sail.

Once we were out in the open sea we started getting thrown all over the place. There were things flying off shelves and people falling over, it was a nightmare. Tony thought it was great, and was more concerned that they had closed the bar, but I didn't like it one bit. It got worse and worse, and we watched the waves lashing on to the side and over the top.

There were people lying on the floor and slumped over tables and chairs, and I suddenly didn't feel too well. I managed to get myself up by holding on to anything I could grab, and made my way to the toilets. I reached the ladies and opened the door to find it full of people being sick, with a river of vomit being swished up and down the floor.

I found a space which somehow wasn't covered in vomit and stood over the sink. After quite a long time a girl came in asking for me and I found out that Tony had sent her in to look for me. She took one look at me and went for a member of staff, who came in and took me out on deck. Alongside me several six-foot blokes were sitting with their sick bags, so I didn't feel quite so daft.

At last the nightmare four hours of the crossing were nearly over. I began to get excited when I saw land. I was beginning to feel a lot better, and it wasn't long before we were back in our vehicles and being led off the ferry and on to Wellington, to a family friend's house. We had directions to the house and found it without problems. The rain was still lashing down and it was blowing a gale, so we had to drive with caution. Once at the house it was wonderful to be inside and warm, and the prospect of being in a proper bed was overwhelming. Our plan was to stay the night, then head to a place called Napier in the morning.

Doreen, the lady we stayed with, was lovely. She was an aunt's friend and was originally from Newcastle, but had moved to New Zealand over thirty years before. She still had her Geordie accent, which was lovely to hear again.

27TH APRIL 2011

In the morning we woke after a fabulous night's sleep. I even had an electric blanket on my side of the bed. The wind had not calmed at all and the rain was making things worse. It was lovely to be in a house in a real bed listening to the rain lashing against the windows. I was quite happy to stay.

We got up and had breakfast while watching the local news on television. They were showing pictures of the damage that had been caused as another tornado had hit Napier in the night. This was exactly where we would have been yesterday if we had not been invited to stay here, and it was where we were supposed to be heading today. We had had yet another lucky escape. The news was telling us that 500 homes in Napier had been evacuated and all roads were closed, so we were stuck in Wellington.

It was actually a great place to be stuck, a nice warm bed, hot water, a toilet and shower and lovely food and hot drinks - it was heaven. As the afternoon wore on the weather wasn't going to get any better, but we realised that if we didn't go out we weren't going to see Wellington. So late that afternoon we decided to venture out.

We drove to the railway station, which was just up the road, and made our way to the ticket desk. We were served by a young girl who had a full beard. I didn't want to look, but I couldn't help it. It was black and about two inches long, but she didn't seem to have noticed.

We caught the local train into the centre of town, where we visited the museum. It was fantastic and totally free (including the bearded lady). We went into a room where we experienced a simulated earthquake, which was pretty terrifying. I certainly wouldn't like to experience one for real. All my tins would be thrown out the cupboard and if the labels aren't facing the front, with my OCD it tips me over the edge. I would probably be more concerned about that than the quake.

We spent hours in the museum, mainly because of the weather. We spoke to a lady inside and asked her directions back to the train station, and she kindly took us back to the station to pick up our car. I couldn't wait to get back to the comforts of bed and a fire.

28TH APRIL

We listened intently to the news, and as it now sounded safer to drive we set off, but we had to drive the west coast instead of the east coast due to the carnage the tornado and landslides had left. It was a nice drive and one we hadn't done before anyway, so we took our time and enjoyed taking in the sights on the way.

We ended up stopping at a place called Wanganui and stayed on a site called the Avro. We were the only ones on the site and had an en suite. I couldn't understand how it was going to work at first, but it was an excellent idea. You pull your van as near as you can to a little brick building, so that when you open the camper van door it leads you straight into your own bathroom. If I ever open a camp site in the UK I will definitely steal this idea.

Time to crack open the wine box after detoxing the last two nights. Made it even better having this en suite, I loved it. Out of all the sites we had been on, this was the first time we had had this facility.

29TH APRIL

We visited the town and had a look around. We got some supplies, in the shape of luxuries like chocolate biscuits. I would have killed in Vietnam or Cambodia for a chocolate biscuit.

We paid a visit to the barber's. I only wanted a trim, but the hairdresser wanted 25 dollars, the robbing git, and the barber was asking 15, so obviously the barber won. He was a huge Maori with loads of traditional tattoos, and he was telling me the significance of them all. They were about his family, his beliefs and his wishes, and he was very interesting. He had arms like totem poles, and when we came out Tony commented on how big he was and said 'He was a big bugger, I wouldn't want to roll about on the floor with him, would you?' He wasn't very happy when I said I wouldn't mind.

We managed to find a second-hand shop, where we bought two pans, and then went into a gorgeous little coffee shop that had hundreds of teapots in the window. Tony ordered a pie and some tea, and when it came he put his tea bag on the side of his plate, which resulted in his pie being covered in tea. To save his embarrassment he told the young waitress that this was the way we eat pie in England. She looked at him unconvinced. I think she thought he had special needs.

When we got back to the site another camper had pulled on near us and the lady from the van ended up in the kitchen with Tony and me. We were quite happy making tea when William and Kate's wedding came on the television. She told us they had been phoning around today asking which site had a television, so she could watch the royal wedding. She was going to be in for the long haul.

It didn't take me long to realise that she was not the full shilling, and possibly related to Derek from the glow worm den. In between the walking up the aisle bit and the cameras scanning over the Beckhams, she told us confidently that the world was going to end next year. I asked her what month (hoping it would be after my birthday), but she said she didn't know the month. I asked her how she knew this, and she said a 'reliable force' had told her. I decided not to pursue it and pretended to be interested in the royal wedding.

By this time she was crooning over Kate Middleton's dress. Ten minutes later she said she was saving up to go to Australia to visit her sister in two years time! I was tempted to remind her that she might want to bring it forward, due to the information that the 'reliable force' had told her, but as she was now chopping mushrooms with a ten-inch knife I decided not to. I had visions of her shouting 'You don't believe me, you heathen, look at Kate's dress, say after me she's beautiful, now repeat, THE WORLD WILL END!' as she backed me into a corner of the kitchen. I carried on watching the wedding, agreeing with her every time she mentioned the dress, Pippa Middleton or William.

The nicest thing about the wedding for me was the fact that Mrs Thatcher was too ill to attend. After a while I made my excuses and left. Tony had already left about an hour before when he realised she was a fruitcake. I got back to the camper and bolted the door in case she decided to wander around in the night taking scalps as trophies with the mushroom knife.

30TH APRIL

When we moved on this morning the mountain tops were covered in snow and the weather was sunny and hot. We had the pleasure of watching a real shepherd rounding up his goats, what a sight to behold. He was whistling and shouting and they were listening to his every command. Heidi was nowhere in sight.

We now reached the largest lake in New Zealand, which is called Lake Taupo. It was formed by the eruption of a volcano which left a huge hole that filled with water. We booked on to a site at a place called De Brett's, and it was out of this world. It's quite a popular stop-off place, so it can be quite busy. The site was built around the hot natural springs, so quite a lot of people visit to experience them.

We decided to get into our swimming gear and go out and experience them for ourselves. It was incredible, lying in water as hot as a bath overlooked by snow-covered mountains. Obviously it's treated and temperature controlled by engineering, otherwise you would just fry to death. In fact before the cooling system was installed some people literally boiled to death. There were private bathrooms where you could bath naked, like film stars.

1ST - 5TH MAY

Today we drove to Rotorua, which was founded in the 14th century by a Maori explorer. Among the first things I learned when I arrived in New Zealand about the Maori language is that Kia-Ora can mean hello or thank you, but not orange juice.

Rotorua is a lovely place, but the smell takes some getting used to. The place stinks of rotten eggs because of the sulphur in the ground. We stayed with our family friends Joe and Margaret, so it was nice to be back in a bed. The simple things in life now seemed to far outweigh everything else, and as we didn't arrive until teatime the first night was spent talking and having a few 'sippers', Joe's word for drinks.

2ND MAY

After a great night's sleep, due to the fact that we were back in a real bed again (and had had a few sippers), we were up ready to start a day of sightseeing. Another great thing about staying with friends was that we got to see some of the sights we could easily have missed. The thermal area in Kuirua Park is there for all to see, but in town it was being advertised as a tour. It's incredible how low the fences are around the boiling hot water and bubbling mud pools. Some areas are quite difficult to see because of the steam. Good for your blackheads though.

I was wearing a silver necklace, and within a day it was completely black and tarnished because of the sulphur. We visited an Anglican church called Ohinemutu, situated right on the lake, gorgeous area but bloody freezing. To be quite honest I could have stayed in the car. In the church there was a huge glass window with Jesus inside the glass, and from the inside of the church when you looked at the window it looked like he was walking on water, which we knew was impossible because only Alan Shearer can do that. Plus he was wearing a Maori coat. (Not Alan Shearer, I don't think he's got a Maori coat.) The weather turned quite windy and cold and it was time to head back home, for, as Joe said, some 'sippers'. Who were we to argue.

185

3RD MAY

Next on the agenda was a visit to the Rotorua Museum and Bath House, where we took the tour of 'taking the cure'. It was once a famous spa offering therapeutic treatments, and people travelled here from all over the world. Some of the treatments involved electrically-wired baths and being buried in mud for hours. It didn't sound very relaxing to me. My sister once buried me in the sand at Whitley Bay, and that was enough to convince me that cremation is the way to go.

We were back in the car and on the move again, this time to visit the coloured lakes. The two lakes we saw were Lake Tikitapu, which is bright blue, and Lake Rotokakahi, which is bright green. The two lakes are right next to each other, separated by a small piece of forest, and if you stand on the hill you can view them side by side.

I spoke to a Maori girl who had a 'mocca' on her face. This was a chin tattoo in the shape of a beard, unlike the lady in the train station who had had a proper beard. I asked her about her tattoo and she told me it represented her three children, and certain marks meant long life and good health. I couldn't help but compare different cultures. She probably wouldn't be allowed in a lot of the bars in Newcastle. The bouncers would be in full 'jobsworth' mode

'But I am Maori and they are traditional Maori markings' she would say.

'Don't care what they are, you're not coming in with those on your face pet.'

'But...'

'No buts, now move on pet.'

Off we went again, this time to the 'buried village', where in the early hours of the morning of June 10th 1886 the Mount Tarawera volcano erupted and for four hours covered the nearby village of Te Walroe with its ash and debris. It also took over 150 people with it.

When you walk on top of the hills nearby and look down, you can still see the tops of a few houses, it's like a scene from The Wizard of Oz. It fascinated me. I could imagine people still in their beds, or food still in the cupboards. Immortalised forever, how fantastic. (Well, obviously not for the poor people who perished.).

On the drive we passed more lakes, Tarawora and Okareka. To be honest a lake's a lake, but if you're a lake spotter this is the place to be and I've seen enough to last me a lifetime.

4TH MAY

This morning Tony and I decided to go into Rotorua town, which was good. We had to sit inside a café to eat because of the smell of rotten eggs. I'm not sure how long it would take me to get used to it, if ever. I had cleaned my necklace, but wasn't going to wear it until after we had left Rotorua. There were very few jewellery shops here, and now I understood why.

The town was nice and the people were very friendly. The Maori people here seemed to have a much more accepted place than the Aborigines of Australia, but the infrastructure was already in place in New Zealand, which made a significant difference.

5TH MAY

My birthday, so no lakes today. We had a great time staying here instead. Eventually, after four nights, we headed off to Hamilton. We were originally going to stay for two nights, but we had such a good time we stayed longer. After a fabulous scenic drive and a few stops along the way, we found a lovely small site and booked on for the night. We walked the short walk into town for something to eat and drink and found a pub that served proper pint glasses, and there was a deal on buy one, get one free, so as you can imagine we took advantage of the offer. The pub was lovely, based on a London pub for some reason. The beer was good and there was a roaring log fire.

Afterwards we walked back across the most beautiful bridge and watched the boats underneath. It was a lovely birthday. This year I had celebrated Christmas day in Vietnam, New Year's Eve in Cambodia and my birthday in New Zealand. Not bad.

6TH MAY

This morning the weather was awful and we had to drive to Auckland. We booked on to another small site, and because the weather was so bad we took the opportunity to sort everything out and bin as much stuff as we could because we were flying to South America in the morning. In the communal kitchen there was a shelf marked 'free stuff', which they have on most sites. It's where people leave their unwanted things and people take what they want. I decided to donate my coat in the hope that I wouldn't need it in South America. Tony said I should keep it just in case, but I bought it from a charity shop and I was sick of wearing it.

After a major sort-out and making sure that Tony had not stuffed anything he shouldn't into my rucksack, we ended the night with a drink and checked some accommodation for when we landed in Chile. Tony was still saying I should take my coat, but after checking the website and the weather it didn't look too cold, so it was destined for the shelf.

7TH MAY

We were up early and again I sneaked into the gents' shower room, because the queue at the ladies was ridiculous. People were complaining, but when I said they should use the gents they looked at me like I was some sort of freak. They were still waiting while I was having breakfast. Who's the fool?

We had sorted everything out and had to drive to the van hire place and return the camper. We got there no bother, we weren't that far away. A quick inspection of the van and we handed over the keys and paperwork and jumped in a taxi to the airport.

Another few hours sitting in the airport. We were now professional flyers. We had accrued quite a few miles since joining the Air Miles club (as opposed to the mile-high club, which we never joined).

How's this for messing your head up. We flew at 4.10 pm and landed at 1 pm, earlier than we had left on the same day! In fact you could fly at certain times on certain flights and never have your birthday. Talk about holding back the years.

Anyway, we got there safely despite the mad time changes and confusion and landed in Chile to find it was bloody freezing. It was 11 degrees, and I desperately wanted my coat back.

Chapter Eleven

CHILE

Tony looked at me shivering in the airport and all he could say was 'I told you'. If I had been a brass monkey I would have been looking for a welder. Great if you were an Eskimo.

We cleared customs and came out of the airport. We had booked some accommodation on the internet, so at least we knew where we were going. We came out of the airport and our first impression of Chile was how poverty-stricken it looked. It was cold, and there was loads of graffiti.

We had directions to the local bus stop from the hostel we were going to, but decided to take a taxi as it was very cheap and hardly anyone spoke English. It was immediately apparent that no one spoke English here, so we knew it was going to be a bit of a problem. After the fiasco in Vietnam when asking for a cup of tea we decided it probably wasn't a good idea to practise our Spanish just yet, until we knew what we were trying to say, as we might have ended up in no man's land.

The driver looked at the piece of paper I had in my hand, on which we had written the name of the hostel. He seemed to understand and drove off. We were in the taxi for about half an hour, quite a long journey. When we got to the hostel the fare was about a quid in our money.

We were staying in a hostel called the Casa Roja and it was

absolutely beautiful. It had originally been a huge palatial mansion. But it was horribly cold and you could see your breath when you spoke.

We had a room in the courtyard and we were a bit worried that it might be noisy, but I was sure that if it got noisy Tony could just stand at the door with his underpants pulled up under his nipples. People would soon move on.

We found out that the staff in the hostel spoke excellent English. They directed us to a whole street of second-hand shops where I could hopefully buy a coat. We dumped our bags in our room, got directions to the shops and set off walking. Outside our hostel was a man standing on the side of the road begging from cars as they stopped at the traffic lights. He was shouting and screaming, and the hostel staff advised us to cross the road to avoid him, which we did. On the walk we passed lots of cafés and bars, all with their windows wide open despite the fact that it was about five degrees outside. At various traffic lights we saw people earning money. A lady dressed as a ballerina would dance when the lights were on red, then go up and down the cars with a hat to collect money. She was beautiful. At another set of lights was a young lad juggling skittles.

We found the street we wanted and I quickly bought a coat, a padded jacket for about a quid, just the job. And even then I think they bumped the price up because we were tourists. We then went into another shop where I bought gloves and a hat and scarf.

While we were in the shop Tony found a lovely thick sweatshirt and said 'I'm going to wash this when I get back to the hostel, how will I wash it?' I said, 'What does it say on it?' He had a look. 'University of California' he said. I wanted to hit him, but I was too cold.

A lady came up to us in the street and gestured that we should have our rucksacks on our chests and not on my back, she was imitating stealing it and running off. She didn't speak any English but we could make out that she was telling us that there are a lot of bag snatchers and thieves. I put the coat straight on and wore it to walk back, but I could feel a sharp pain in my ribs and couldn't find out what it was. When we got back to the hostel there had been a pin in the side of the coat that had pierced my skin, so I now needed a new jumper because mine was covered in blood.

Back at the hostel Tony got talking to a lad who was staying there. Ten minutes into the conversation it became clear that the lad was a Scientologist. Tony and I were listening to him talking about how you don't need doctors or medication, just prayer and hope. I was secretly hoping he was going to get bitten by one of the dogs, as the ones in this area were not inoculated. We made our excuses and left, and on the way out, with a dead straight face, Tony asked him if he had any Paracetamol. Just before the lad could say anything Tony said 'ah no, it's OK, I've got some'.

When bedtime came we had to do star jumps before we could get in because it was so cold.

8TH MAY

Today we went on a photographic and walking tour, which was free. The idea was that if you liked the tour you tipped the girl however much you wanted. Great, I thought, I might get some tips on taking the best pictures, not to mention Tony and his point-and-shoot theory.

Off we went to the Santa Lucia Hill and the Paris and Londres neighbourhoods, which were gorgeous. The views from the top of the hill were lovely. I asked how I could take a picture if the sunlight was in the way and another girl said she was also wondering the same, and she said she didn't know. Tony said 'just point and shoot and if it comes out then great' She said 'Yes I agree'. I couldn't believe Tony was now somehow giving other people tips, after all the fights we'd had over the camera. I asked her to take a photograph of Tony and me, and we weren't even in position before she was walking back to me with the camera. All this did was support Tony's notion that you just point and shoot.

Again on two occasions strangers came up to us and in broken English gestured for us to keep our bags in front and not on our backs. There were police every hundred yards or so. We saw a young lad doing some graffiti and the local policeman gave him a good whack with his baton. People were patting the policeman on the back and kicking the vandal up the arse. Proactive and reactive policing all in one.

We called into a place for lunch. Santiago town centre was very much like any other big city, lots of shops, people, cars, and hundreds of stray dogs everywhere. The dogs are looked after by the people and they go everywhere, wearing collars to say they have been inoculated.

On the local bus we wondered why there were people standing when it looked like there was a seat near the back of the bus. We soon found out that there was a large black and white dog occupying two seats. Apparently lone females at night will have a dog to walk alongside and protect them.

9TH MAY

We went out exploring again and watched the various acts performing for money at the traffic lights. The dogs don't have to perform, they just lie about and shit everywhere. No one harms them and they seem to be well accepted. There is a huge university area here in Santiago which is very populated. The whole city is massively crowded. It's very commercialised, with some expensive shops and loads of cheap clothing and swap shops.

Personally I couldn't wait to get out of the big city and head off to see the real Chile. I hadn't expected it to be so cold. Even the dogs had coats on.

The only way to get warmed up was to go into a café, or so we thought. Either way we had to go and eat, so we pointed at a picture of chicken and chips on the wall, thinking it would be easy. That was, until a bowl of onion soup arrived. Since when has chicken and chips looked like a bowl of onion soup? I gave up and ate it, and it was bloody horrible. I'm not even convinced it was onion.

10TH MAY

Got up this morning and stayed under the hot shower for what seemed like ages. I would have stayed under longer, but they were communal and there were people waiting. I was starving after my onion soup, but due to the cold and the number of layers I had on I could hardly get close to the cooker to make some toast. When a young girl came into the kitchen wearing a pair of leggings and a T shirt, I stood looking at her in total amazement, you could literally see your own breath it was so cold.

Within minutes all the young lads seemed to want to cook. It wasn't until she turned around you could see how prominent her camel's toe was. Put me right off my toast.

We had decided to check out today in the hope that the next place might be a bit warmer. So after a quick cup of tea we got the bus to a place called Vina del Mar. It was cold on the bus, but they still had the air conditioning on, for God's sake.

A few hours later we stepped off the bus at our destination and were practically jumped on by people wanting to carry our bags and take us to a hostel. It was chaos, people shoving each other and pushing past. It was like a sale in Primark. We ignored them, after saying several times 'no thanks'.

As it turned out it was only about a ten-minute walk to the Rokaman Hotel where we were heading. It had looked great on the internet and had good reviews. It seemed to be in a good location. As we knocked on the glass door we could see someone on the reception desk, and he quickly came and welcomed us in. He was wearing a coat, hat and scarf and had a very purple nose. We soon realised that there was no heating of any description anywhere. I just about started crying and wanted to stab myself.

We got booked in anyway, and he spoke a little English so I took my chances and asked him if there was any heating. He looked at me as if I had asked him for a limb, so I took it as a no. Thankfully we were given a room on the top floor, because at least by the time we got upstairs we had a bit of a sweat on.

We decided to venture outside and have a nosey around, mainly because it was warmer out than in. We had to go shopping, as we needed some bottled drinking water. We went into a couple of shops, and in each shop there was a guard at each aisle standing on a chair with a rifle in his hand. To be a shoplifter here you must have to be desperate. I wouldn't want to get shot for a tin of beans, and I wouldn't want to be standing next to someone who was shoplifting. How many innocent bystanders get accidentally shot, I wondered?

A sales assistant rushed after us as we entered the shop and pushed a basket in my hand, indicating that it might look suspicious if we didn't have one. I put my gloves in the basket, not thinking, and at the checkout thankfully they realised they were well worn and they didn't charge me for them. I wouldn't have argued with an AK47 pointed at me, though personally I think it was a bit over the top. It would be like getting the electric chair for shoplifting from the Pound Shop. Having said that, the batteries to power the chair would be cheap.

I was terrified to pick anything up in case the guards thought I was trying to steal it. I was more worried when I saw a fat guard, and I was hoping the chair wouldn't give out under him, I had images of being peppered with bullets, or worse still him shooting a hole in the new hot-water bottle I had in my basket. I also bought a huge tin of Oust because I knew that the bars and cafes here were thick with smoke.

We found a bar called Syphilis (or at least that's what the sign looked like). As we went in it was like 'Tonight Matthew I'm going to be...', but we eventually saw a barmaid through the plumes of smoke and ordered a beer, which was dirt cheap and good. If I thought I was going to be in a nice warm pub I was sadly mistaken, as now we had to sit next to the open window to get away from the smoke. Back at the room I sprayed our clothes and did a few star jumps again in order to keep warm.

11TH MAY

We visited the local park today, which was lovely, but we didn't stay too long as there were gangs of undesirable people lurking about and we felt a bit nervous. Thankfully we didn't get followed, but we did get a few strange looks. Maybe they were thinking 'They're wearing our clothes'. We saw at least fifty or sixty dogs in the park, or four-legged shit machines as Tony calls them.

We walked back through town and found a shop that sold hot bread - well it looked like bread, but I'm not actually sure what it was, it tasted a bit like dumplings. We ate them anyway, because believe me it was better than what was on the menus in some of the cafés.

There was a football match showing on the telly in every pub and café, and we were the only non-smokers in Chile, or so it seemed. We went into a bar called Dublin and it was all painted in green and depicting Ireland. We never did find out the connection. The smoke was horrendous. With his glasses on and his raspy throat Tony could now pass for Deirdre Barlow.

We had a few beers and went back to the hostel via the local kebab shop. We got a wrap each, and I'm not sure what was in it but we were hungry and it looked edible enough and actually tasted not too bad. I had really been looking forward to the food in South America, because I thought it would be chilli and fajitas and stuff, but it wasn't even recognisable, except the chicken and chips, and even then they brought us onion soup.

There was a man in the shop opposite sitting in candlelight, I wasn't sure if it was for the warmth or the ambience. I couldn't make out what kind of shop it was and it was too cold to go and have a look. I made a conscious effort to remember to have a good look tomorrow. After our wrap we headed around the corner to the hostel and ran up and down the stairs a few times before completing twenty star jumps to warm up for bed. I was wondering if the Chileans thought this was English foreplay.

12TH MAY

Twenty more star jumps in the morning and we were ready to go for breakfast. My hot water bottle did the job, but I'm not sure what kind of rubber it was made from as I was now smelling like a giant condom. The breakfast was a bread roll and a knob of butter that definitely wasn't the spreadable type. A pot of tea warmed us up a bit.

Because the hostel was so cold we had no choice but to go out. We had seen some huge houses on top of the hill just beside the hostel, so we decided to walk to them and have a look. They were pretty amazing. They were heavily fenced off, so we couldn't get too close, and a few had huge guard dogs which were definitely not friendly. We found a lovely café where we stood in the queue for about fifteen minutes. We couldn't speak any Spanish but we tried to order a pizza anyway. There was much confusion, but we succeeded, or so we thought, until it arrived and it was the size of a saucer.

We soon found ourselves back at the bread/dumpling shop. After a few portions we called into the Dublin place for a beer. On the way back I decided to check out the shop that I hadn't been able to make out the night before. It was dark now, so I put my hands to my face and pressed it against the window.

I got the shock of my life. It was a funeral parlour, and three coffins were on display with bodies in them. Personally I think they had put too much rouge on the woman, as she looked like she could have starred in a remake of Whatever Happened to Baby Jane. They didn't look very old, either that or the cold had done them the world of good. I wondered if the lady had been shot in the chemist while trying to buy a deodorant. Cold as she was, she still looked warmer than I felt.

The undertaker came to the door and invited me in. I don't know if he thought I was coming to view or if he had a new customer, I must certainly have looked cold enough for a coffin.

After that little episode and the sightings of more armed police than Northumbria have on a manhunt, we went in search of something to eat. So far all we had succeeded in ordering was a miniature pizza and two dumplings, so we were starving. We found a little place and went in, and the game started again, with us pointing and guessing. To our pleasant surprise we got a plate of chips with bread and butter. Believe me, when you have been trying to order something simple for days this was heaven.

We went back to Syphilis for a few beers, and sat watching people coming and going. After a visit to the ladies I found that there were two toilets, one with a saloon door that was out of order and one with no door that had a large turd staring up at me. I was curious to find the female that had passed it without an epidural. I would rather have wet myself than have to use these facilities. Back in the bar, nursing a full bladder, streaming eyes and a raspy throat, I decided it was time to move on. Thankfully I would be able to go to the toilet when we got back to our room, as the thought of doing star jumps with a full bladder was not a good one. Jump, squirt, jump, squirt, jump, squirt.

13TH MAY

Today we had the pleasure of travelling by local bus back to the Casa Roja hostel, as we had decided to go along with eight other people and trek the Patchamama Trail through the Atacama Desert, which would take us a week. We had to take our time so that we could acclimatise to the altitude. A large Alsatian-type dog gave up his seat for me on the bus, which I thought was very nice of him.

On arrival at the hostel we had the advantage of already knowing how basic the restaurants around here were, so we put our name down for the hostel BBQ that evening. I'm not a huge fan of meat so I opted for the vegetarian option, thinking I would just have some of Tony's chicken if it looked OK. The idea of a vegetarian at a BBQ is quite funny anyway.

We didn't bother going out to the shops as we had already seen what was on offer and we weren't missing anything. We just caught up with some emails we needed to send and chilled out for a while. It was already late afternoon after our bus ride, so we stayed in our room.

We had asked for a room inside the main building this time, hoping it would be a bit warmer. We were given a nice room and it actually was warmer.

We headed downstairs, armed with the beer we had bought from the hostel, and headed for the BBQ in the courtyard. Not long after arriving I heard a lad say 'Who's the fucking arsehole vegetarian?' rolling his eyes to the sky. I thought about saying 'Hey it's me dickhead', but I decided to ignore it and tried to blend in.

No chance. Five minutes later the chef shouted 'Can the vegetarian come first please, vegetarians first, then girls, then boys, vegetarian come forward please'. I walked the walk of shame for my salad and cheese and onion pizza while secretly salivating over the chicken and other meat. What made it worse was that I was wearing a woolly jumper and Jesus sandals. I think people were avoiding me in case I suggested we make dreamcatchers and dance around trees all night. In reality I just wanted to eat and get pissed so I would sleep.

As I was walking round the table I was aware of everyone watching me and I could hear the girls saying 'We can't go up till the vegetarian's finished' as if I was going to infect them. I sat and pretended to be enjoying my cardboard pizza and didn't even dare look at Tony's chicken.

When the BBQ was finished a few of the young ones went off to a club while we stayed behind and finished the drinks. I was nearly over my humiliation when we started talking to a young lad who said to us 'I think it's great that you are backpacking. You can only do it twice in your life, when you're young and when you're old, like you guys' I could have hit him there and then. He did look about fourteen, so he might have had a point.

14TH MAY

Thanks to a load of morons we didn't get much sleep last night. Some of the people obviously thought it was a huge laugh knocking on doors and running up and down corridors until six in the morning. I was hoping one of the shop security guards had to be up for work and would open up his AK47 in the corridor and take a few of them out. I did think about complaining the next morning, but I was worried they might lodge my complaint in the 'vegetarian section' and people would think I was just a pain in the arse.

Day one, and the start of the trail. We were first on. The other eight passengers joined us at different locations. They were a canny crowd, but Tony and I were by far the oldest. Our guide was called Yethsen, with great emphasis on the 'th', so each time you said it you spat over the nearest person. I asked if he had a nickname and he said no, just Yethsen, and sprayed the 'th' in my face, great.

When everyone introduced themselves it was clear that we had been lucky enough to get a good group. There was a couple from Australia, five young Dutch kids and a single Australian lad. We were going to be together for a week, sharing accommodation and spending hours on the bus together, so this was a bonus. After a few hours' drive, when we passed through some of the most amazing scenery, we arrived at our first stop, a place named Pichidangu (it means 'small raft', in case you're interested). It was a lovely little town with only 1200 inhabitants, of which about 700 were dogs. Real dogs, not ugly women, thought we saw quite a few of those too.

Second stop was a place named La Serena, which is Chile's second largest city. It's very pretty in places with its neo-colonial architecture, a legacy of President Gabriel Gonzalez Videla, who was born here (I didn't know who he was either). Our hostel had no heating, which didn't really come as that much of a shock, and was basic to say the least.

When we opened the door several small, unidentifiable, fast-running things made a dash for it across the floor, probably looking for warmth. There were no towels provided, so we had to go in search of one. After we had checked in a few of us went to have a look around the town, which was bustling mad with street markets and people in the streets selling everything from clothing to food that they had cooked. Most of it was vegetables that we didn't recognise and didn't look or smell very good.

Yethsen had told us to be careful when we were out in the street and to stay together, emphasising safety in numbers. We managed to dodge our way through the market and eventually found a towel for a low price. We dodged and pushed our way back to the hostel and made a noise outside the room before we entered to give the things that were running around the floor time to get out. It looked like we would have to do a few star jumps before bed again, so anything underfoot was going to be squashed anyway.

15TH MAY

After his shower I wasn't sure if Tony had hypothermia or it was my eyes. He looked like he had a blue beard, and all his hair was covered in blue fluff. The towel was soaked, and it hadn't even dried him. We'd bought the most useless towel in the world. I had to resort to my big T shirt. I knew it would come in handy.

It was seven in the morning and the streets were already filling up with people setting up stalls and markets. After finding a shop that sold something resembling food, we bought what we thought was a sausage roll. After 'breakfast' we left La Serena and headed towards Bahia Inglesa, the English Village. It's named after an English pirate and only 135 people live here. We visited a tiny village called Punta De Choros, where we boarded a wooden boat that looked like it might have been made by Noah himself. The good thing was that we got a life-jacket each. It was like the jacket you see on the demonstration on a flight, with a whistle and torch attached, presumably in case there's a disco on the island where you're washed up on.

The wind was blowing and the sea was pretty choppy, but it calmed down once we hit open water. My experience of the ferry in New Zealand was flooding back to me, but it was OK after a while. We passed the tiniest penguins, only about six inches high, and loads of seals, and a pod of dolphins swam alongside the boat showing off, we could almost touch them. They were so close to the boat that we could actually hear them breathing and making dolphiny noises.

Suddenly the skipper started talking frantically with his mate, and they turned the boat round and headed at great speed in a different direction. There were concerned looks and people talking under their breath. Then one of the men gestured for us to look, and there in front of us was a blue whale. It passed right by us. It was one of the most magnificent sights we have ever seen. We were very lucky to see it, they're the biggest animal that has ever existed on Earth. Everyone was speechless.

We were staying in a cabin in the middle of the desert for the next two nights along with three other people. It was tiny, but cosy. The walls were paper-thin and trying to keep the conversation going while Tony went to the bathroom was a challenge. The three others decided to chill out and have a bottle of mineral water each, so Tony and I did the same. Not!

16TH MAY

Spending the morning on a freezing cold windswept beach was not my idea of fun. It was very picturesque though, as no one else was around for miles. Even the stray dogs were shivering. We visited Coplapo, where the Chilean miners who had recently been rescued from a mining accident lived. The mine was only five kilometers from us.

We went for lunch to a small town nearby and sampled a Chilean empanadas, which is a deep-fried pasty-type thing with a choice of fillings. They are all beef, so if you don't like beef you're pretty much stuffed. The menu board, when translated to us by Yethsen, was beef and onion, beef and cheese, beef and garlic or just beef. We were having a barbecue in the evening and the bus driver was cooking it for us, so we decided to just chill out and wait. I wasn't going for the vegetarian option this time.

There was nothing around us for miles and miles except desert and a few wooden huts built for people passing through. We had been told to meet in the 'casino' and were told that if we walked with our torch towards the desert road we would see it. After a short walk we came across a wooden hut which turned out to be the casino, don't ask why. We ate and drank and got merry and soon found out that our guide wanted to eat, drink and be Mary. We had a good laugh all round and a good night. I taught the Dutch kids to play pigeon toss, which they had never heard of. My mis-spent youth sprang to the surface yet again.

17TH MAY

As we headed deeper into the desert the weather was getting hotter. The conversation on the bus was good and we all got on well. We trekked across the driest part of the desert, a place that has seen no rain for fifty years. The scenery was breathtaking, with the Andes on one side and desert as far as you could see on the other.

We passed through a part of the desert that holds an old abandoned cemetery. It is literally in the middle of nowhere, and hours and hours from any civilisation. Because of the combination of temperature and low humidity decomposition of the bodies is slowed down. Sometimes the high winds expose the secrets of the graves. It is not particularly nice to see hair and bones lying in the earth. But the fresh flowers on some of the graves showed that people obviously still travel here.

We got back on the bus and drove for miles. I can't stress enough how fantastic it felt to be travelling through the desert. We arrived at a sculpture by the artist Mario Irarrazabal, called the 'Hand of the Desert'. His thinking behind it was apparently to give a 'hand' to the people, but personally if I thought someone was going to give me a hand I wouldn't expect a huge concrete one. I bet there were a few surprised faces. Apparently the artist has one on a smaller scale in

Barcelona. Tony took some photographs and it instantly became the palm of the desert.

After more travelling on the bus and endless sand, sand and more sand, we got to a place called Antofagasta, which means 'hidden copper'. It's a massive place. This area is blessed with the clearest skies in the world, with no more than twenty cloudy days a year. It also boasts the largest radio telescope array in the world, which is called ALMA, not for some unknown lady out there but because it stands for the Atacama Large Millimetre/Submillimeter Array. Which to you and me is a big telescope.

On the coast there is a huge natural arch in the sea, similar to the one that was at South Shields before it collapsed. The naturally-coloured cliffs that surrounded the arch were much more spectacular, and all the birdshit made it look complete.

Our hostel that night was a total dive, but OK for one night I suppose. After a few beers it looked pretty palatial and made us realise just how good the beer was in Chile.

18TH MAY

Today we travelled for hours through more desert, the scenery getting better and better. We arrived at a place called Banquedano, where we visited an abandoned train depot. After the collapse of the railroads the trains were left there, as they couldn't be transported anywhere. The tracks had been removed, so the trains were standing on the little piece of track under them. The whole place felt very eerie. It's a train spotters dream, or rather a nightmare if they would rather see them up and running. Because of the low humidity the trains have resisted corrosion. There's been some vandalism, but with a little TLC and some WD40 they could be practically up and running.

Next stop was the Tropic of Capricorn, the imaginary line round the world that marks the place where the tropics begin. We stopped at a spot where a monument had been erected to signify this. It's just a spot - you can't see anything - but it's also an indicator of the change in altitude.

The drive across here was quite bumpy as we drove for miles along salt compacted roads. We couldn't resist getting out and tasting the road and its true, it was pure salt. It was incredible to think that the whole place was just salt and it's only now a road because of the vehicles that cross.

We were now 2400 metres above sea level, but so far everyone was feeling OK. We stopped at a tiny village where only 400 people lived, again with about 700 dogs. It was just a street lined with very basic shacks. There was also a tiny church, which it was lovely. There was an oasis where we could swim, but when I saw the green algae I decided not to bother. Yethsen said it was a type of seaweed, but then he had also said the last hostel was good. When Tony got out of the water, everywhere he needed a shave was covered in sticky green algae. Me coming out with a green bikini line would not be a good look, trust me.

On the other side of the oasis was a tiny one-horse town that had been abandoned years ago, to this day no one knows why. It was very spooky. You could see furniture, an old rocking chair on a porch rocking slightly in the breeze and clothing still hanging on lines, yet not a living soul to be seen. I was hoping their disappearance had nothing to do with swimming in the oasis.

The light was beginning to fade now and we had to move on to the Valle De La Luna, or Moon Valley. It's called that because of its resemblance to the surface of the moon, with its different stratifications and the salt formations caused by natural environmental changes. It is also a flamingo reserve. We waited for over an hour, but it was worth it. We could see the Cordillera and Andes.

It was a truly spectacular sight. It didn't take long for the sun to go down, and once it did the changes started happening before our eyes. Everything went red for a few minutes, then blue, and finally purple.

A huge group of flamingos flew over us and the outline of them against the purple sky was amazing.

We drove in the dark to our next destination, San Pedro. We arrived in darkness and the whole place was pitch black. We could just make out some activity by the light of candles. As we passed a group of men sitting on a dirt track we could make out the whites of their eyes. You could hear dogs barking, but it was impossible to see how many there were.

We arrived at the hostel and were shown to the room by candlelight, feeling along the wall as we went. I could feel the plaster being knocked off. Soon we had power, and as the light came on we had a quick scan around the room. It had looked better with the light off. But we were staying here for two nights, so we had to make the most of it.

We armed ourselves with torches and coats and ventured out. It was cold. We soon hit the main area of town and found that there were no roads, just dirt tracks, and no shop fronts. It was very unspoilt and raw. I loved it. This is what I had wanted to see, the real Chile.

There were men on horseback and roaring fires in crudely-made grates. The power was on and off so many times we couldn't count, but it added to the ambience of the place. It was like the Bonanza and the High Chaparral combined. We could hear the distant sound of horses' hooves and smell the leather from the saddle shops.

We had to go to bed by candlelight, not out of romance but because of the power cuts. I think the water is heated by candlelight too, and my skin went a nice shade of purple under the freezing water.

19TH MAY

We went to visit the Laguna Cejar, a lagoon of dense salty water. After about an hour's drive across the desert, on very bumpy roads, we arrived. We had to get changed on the bus, then it was a five-minute walk down to the lake. On entering the water it was quite difficult to walk because of the salt. Sinking was impossible, and when you stood up you bobbed up and down like a giant cork. The worst thing was coming out of the water and being covered in white chalky salt. It took ages to wash off and was virtually impossible to get out of our hair.

Next we went to the salt caves, where we had to crawl in tiny confined spaces. I got so far in and then found it too claustrophobic, so after the image of the Chilean miners flashed through my mind I bailed out. Tony and the rest of the group kept going, and when they finally emerged at the other end they all said the spaces had got smaller and smaller, so I was pleased I hadn't gone on. Instead I walked, or attempted to walk, up the dunes to take some pictures. Afterwards Yethsen spat out the information to the group that it was not safe to climb the dunes as a while ago someone was buried alive when the sand collapsed.

We were right in the Andes Mountains now and I couldn't help thinking of the survivors from the plane crash featured in the film Alive. They now live in Paraguay, and the cowboy who found them lives in Chile. We passed through his village on the way here. When you stand and look out and see how vast it is, it seems incredible that anyone could have walked that far. We watched the sunset over the mountains and it was beautiful.

20TH MAY

Today we completed our trek through the Atacama Desert and spent time reflecting on all the magnificent sights we had witnessed. We got back to the hostel and checked out, and then we all went out for dinner at a small restaurant in town. After dinner we had to travel to Arica, on the border with Peru.

We were lucky to catch a bus at half eight that night. It took us ten hours to get to the border. On the bus we met the five Dutch kids from the group. The journey was comfortable, with massive seats that reclined enough for a good sleep. We were all pretty knackered with the trek, so we were happy to be on the bus.

It was half six in the morning when we arrived at the nearest point to the border and quickly realised that it was not the safest place to be. We had safety in numbers though, and all stuck close together. Two of the girls spoke Spanish, so we were able to find a couple of taxis. We had to hurry through the streets and get into the taxis.

After two hours in the taxis we reached the border, where our taxi door was opened by a large man wielding a very large gun. We were ushered out and told to wait. He spoke to another man and then shouted at us to get out our passports. We weren't sure if at this point we were going to be asked for money, but he took our passports and gestured us through while pointing his gun at us. We were pretty scared by this time and I was more than a bit worried, as he still had his gun pointed at me and he looked like he meant business.

We cleared passport control, which was basically a hut in the middle of nowhere with menacing-looking guards with guns. No one argued with anyone and we went on our way. We had made it to the border, and now we had to cross it. We had to travel by another taxi to Tacna, because it was not safe to cross any other way and only designated cars could cross. We were hoping we didn't have a driver who was moonlighting, as we didn't fancy being shot for someone who was making a quick buck on the side.

Chapter Twelve

PERU

After a nervous drive into Tacna, where we passed many armed police and poverty-stricken landscape scenes, we realised that it was not a good place to be if you valued your life and your belongings. We decided that when we got there we would try and catch another bus to Arequipa, which was another six hours. We were lucky enough to get a couple of seats on the bus for Arequipa, and settled down for the journey.

An hour into the journey to Arequipa, the bus was stopped by armed police, who came aboard shining torches in our faces and having a look around the bus. They looked quite satisfied that we were travelling as tourists. As we looked out of the windows at the desolate landscape and the poverty, we were getting a bit worried about where we were going to stay. When we got there we quickly realised that this was not a good place to be either, and definitely not safe, so we decided to wait another five hours to catch another bus to Cusco, which was going to take thirteen hours travelling through the night.

We were knackered, but we had to keep going. By this time we were so tired we weren't tired, if that makes sense. We were like maniacs suffering from sleep deprivation.

The bus station was quite big, with a few café-type places and small shops. There were people everywhere selling baked bread and savoury snacks. I don't know to this day what was in them, but they looked and tasted OK.

The area here was pretty intimidating, and we had to make a conscious effort to guard our belongings. The bus eventually arrived and we got on, sitting upstairs again. We were totally knackered by this time, and I just wanted to get my head down and try to get to sleep.

As soon as the bus moved off a kid behind me started kicking my chair. It took all my self-control not to turn round and punch him in the face, kid or not. As soon as his mother went to the toilet I turned round and stared at him with a clenched fist and my teeth clenched together. He got the message and didn't kick my chair any more, though I think his mother was concerned about how quiet he was. The way I was feeling I would have punched her as well.

We arrived in Cusco at 5 am and found the whole place alive with sellers and people rushing around. The last thing you want when you have been travelling for umpteen hours is people in your face. We got off the bus, grabbed our bags and jumped into a car that resembled a taxi. We had booked a hostel on line and showed him the name and address.

We got in the back, and as he pulled away the bottom of the car scraped on the ground. He stopped the car and without speaking any English, ordered Tony into the front, gesturing that we were too fat. Off we went again in the car, which was like something out of the Flintstones and probably worth about two quid if scrapped for parts. As he drove, Tony and I sat with our mouths open. We couldn't believe how rough and poor this area looked.

It was now 5 am. We were driving uphill towards a bridge at the top where we could turn left or right. The traffic didn't seem to have any order and it was impossible to guess which lane he was in, if any. On the approach to the top we saw a woman trying to jump off the bridge, while several people pulled her back. She was screaming and shouting and the drunks under the bridge were shouting at her to shut up, or at least that's what it sounded like. The driver turned to us and made a drinking gesture, indicating that she was drunk.

According to the website, our hostel was right in the heart of Cusco, where you are 'guaranteed to see real life'. They got that right. The whole place looked like a war zone, complete with areas that looked as if they had just been shelled. We got out the taxi and were a stone's throw from the woman who was still trying to jump, and we were getting looked at by a few characters.

The hostel was surrounded by a ten-foot fence, complete with locked gates. We stood and rang the bell and the manager came out to meet us. He then proceeded to open the several locks on the gate and let us in. As he was talking to us he was busy putting the locks back on, so either way it looked very much like we were staying.

The altitude was incredible. The air was very thin and we were both struggling for breath. We quickly realised why people have to stay in Cusco for a few days to acclimatise before travelling on. The inside of the hostel was quite nice and the manager was friendly. He showed us an oxygen bottle in the reception, which we could use any time we needed it. I was tempted to have a blast when he said our room was on the second floor.

We were shown to our room and found that there was no heating, yet again, and just to make sure the room was aired the windows were wide open. We were in dire need of a shower after travelling for a zillion hours on numerous buses, and were pleasantly surprised to find the water was red hot. I stood under the shower, which was fantastic.

We were hungry and tired, but anxious to check the place out. The manager spoke great English and told us to be careful when we went out because there were a lot of homeless people and people desperate for money, though overall he said it was a pretty safe place.

He told us they need tourism, so the police and locals don't take kindly to anyone threatening or mistreating travellers. I wasn't really bothered about the threats, it was more the odd stray bullet.

We got changed and went out for a walk anyway, because our need for food now felt greater than our safety. We came across a shop that had a pig roasting on a spit, which reminded me of the last spit roasting I saw, but that's another story. Anyway the hot pork sandwiches were delicious and massive, all for the huge price of about twenty pence. We found the people were warm and generous and first impressions didn't do Cusco justice. We passed a few places that took in laundry, basically a few women sitting in back lanes around huge tubs of soapy water washing clothes. There was no hazard tape or white suits, so they probably wouldn't take in Tony's socks.

We had only been out walking at a slow pace for an hour and were both seriously out of breath. The air was so thin and cold. But the people here were so warm. They had burnt-looking cheeks and were all in traditional dress, while the kids had painted cheeks that looked as if they had been coloured on.

There was a huge festival in the town square, with so many dancers and costumes. I suddenly didn't feel too well with altitude sickness, which makes a change as Tony says it's usually attitude sickness with me.

23RD MAY

After falling into bed and sleeping right through, I woke up feeling like shit. I thought I might have picked up a bug. Along with altitude sickness I was throwing up. The manager gave me some oxygen and me some coca leaves, which he said I needed to eat as they helped with altitude sickness. I had a few cups of coca tea and after an hour or so started to feel a little better. All I wanted to do was sleep.

24TH MAY

Had ten minutes of oxygen and five cups of coca tea this morning and felt a lot better. We walked into town after breakfast. We had thought of moving hostels, but decided to stay put as it was very friendly, and once we got used to the smell of the streets and the poverty it was quite a nice place to be.

On the main street we passed the bank and watched the guards outside with their guns cocked and their fingers on the triggers. If anything happened they would have a good aim, or they would definitely take a few out in the crossfire. We sat in the main square, where the sellers and beggars were congregating. The park attendant was stopping anyone from walking on the grass, which seemed to be a bigger offence than one of the security guards accidentally shooting someone.

We were approached by one of the sellers, aged about twelve, trying to sell us both a hat. We politely refused and he went on his way. They don't hassle you if you say no thanks, they go, unlike other places.

Ten minutes later Tony decided he did in fact want the hat, so we went off in search of the seller. We thought we would show a bit of loyalty. He was wearing a red coat, and each time we saw him he disappeared round a corner. This went on for about two hours, like the film Don't Look Now, except that we weren't in Venice.

We gave up looking and went for a beer, then as we sat on a balcony overlooking the square we spotted him. We watched him for a while, and when I thought it was OK I raced down the stairs and caught up with him. I had forgotten about the altitude, and I was like a wheezing asthmatic when I caught him. He was a cheeky bugger and said I had to pay more because of our change of mind. So much for our loyalty! I eventually gave him six sols, which is about one pound fifty, and returned to the pub with two hats. Incidentally they now sell them in the Pound Shop, but they won't be as good as ours and ours are original.

25TH MAY

This morning we got up early for our journey up to Machu Picchu. We didn't book the Inca Trail, which would have taken us four days. Instead we travelled up by bus and train.

The journey up was incredible. The train cut through forest and unspoiled landscape (apart from the train) and because of the precarious drop at times it occasionally had to stop before setting off again. Each time it stopped sellers appeared at the window with their wares and trade bargains.

The train climbed the track and then we boarded a bus which took us through the mountains. As we passed houses the locals waved at us. Apparently some like the train, while others hate it. We passed a house right next to the track where an elderly man and his wife were working. They had a goat, some chickens, a pig and a horse's head on a stick. The significance of the horse's head remains a mystery. This must be real hard work, no electricity, no running water and no gas.

Bears the size of humans, along with pumas, are still seen in this area, but unfortunately we didn't see either. Maybe the horse's head was to stop the bears approaching, or it was the Godfather's holiday let.

When the train stopped we had to board a bus up the mountain. I couldn't understand how we had left Cusco, which is 3300 metres above sea level, and travelled upwards to Machu Picchu, 2400 metres above sea level. I still can't figure it out.

The climb in the bus was quite terrifying and I had to stop myself from looking out of the window, where there was a sheer drop. Tony said we should have sat on the other side because the drop was on our side, but I said to him that if the bus fell off the side of the mountain it would be irrelevant which side you were sitting on.

When we reached the top we found we needed our passports. After we had explained that we had not been told to bring them with us, they eventually let us in. Personally I think they take passports and names of people in case the bus goes over the cliff.

Another short climb, this time on foot, and we reached the top to be met by the most breathtaking sight. The 'Hidden City' was beautiful, so green and totally mesmerizing. It was hard to believe that all those stones had been carried up by hand and no cement or mortar was used. The stones were cut with such precision and joined together so you couldn't get a piece of paper between them.

Contrary to popular belief, there is no evidence that the Spanish ever invaded, or that precious stones and jewels were found here, although in 1995 a gold bracelet was found buried and a tree has been planted in the spot.

The belief is that the Incas left Machu Picchu to prevent it being invaded, and never returned. We were told that Machu Picchu only has two seasons, a dry and a wet season, unlike Britain, which has all the seasons in one afternoon. We have the rainy season, the pissing-down season, the snow season, the hailstone season and the summer, which usually lasts only three days and never on a weekend.

As we began walking it got hotter and the sun started to beat down. I turned and said to Tony, who I thought was beside me, 'Glad we didn't put our hats on, we would have looked like a right couple of knobs'. When I turned round I saw Tony was at the other side of the group. I had been talking to a young couple wearing matching beanie hats.

Five minutes later I spotted a couple with a baby and said to Tony. 'Who the hell would bring a baby up Machu Picchu?'

'Yeah, they're great climbers' he said.

'Eh?'

'The babies, the baby llamas' Tony said.

Forget it. I blame the altitude!

We spent the afternoon there and saw the whole of the hidden village before heading back down the mountain to catch our train. The bus was even scarier going downhill. One false move by the driver and we might have reached the bottom quicker than we wanted to. I know he had probably done it a million times, but that's just when you get complacent.

I was glad to see the bottom of the mountain anyway. We had a while to wait, so we got a beer and were entertained by a blind violinist. We were hungry and thirsty, and as we were in Peru the roasted guinea pig looked good enough to eat. Not much meat on it though.

26TH MAY

Saw the most ingenious thing today on a beggar. Someone had apparently given him a pair of trousers, the ones you zip the legs off to make into shorts. He had zipped the legs off because he was short anyway and was wearing the bottom part of the legs as arm warmers. I could hear his speech in the dragon's den as Theo was debating how much of his business he wanted. I thought it was great and gave him a couple of sol.

There were a lot of people gathering in the square and it didn't take long to realise that they were quite an angry crowd. From the literature that was pinned on the walls we could make out that they were demonstrating against a candidate running in the Peru elections. She was the daughter of an ex-dictator who had committed genocide. It was a good enough reason to be protesting, but we still made the decision to get out of the square pretty quick. We didn't fancy getting caught up in it if it went tits up.

27TH MAY

There was yet another festival on today. I suppose when your surroundings are as depressing as this, the more festivals the better. We took a local bus out into no man's land to see the countryside, and no surprises, there were plenty of stray dogs roaming around. When you see the way the houses have been built into the hills it is not surprising when you hear of a landslide demolishing 500 houses. They look like they were built in half an hour by someone on their dinner hour. Kids could demolish a whole row just trying to retrieve a football. One slip and they would go down like dominoes.

Further up the village we saw a street entertainer, although personally I thought the word entertainer was one he had made up himself. On the board advertising the show was a picture of a man putting things in his mouth. We couldn't make out what the objects were and couldn't read the board, so we decided we would watch the show. There was a drum roll from a battery-operated cassette player. The entertainer now had a captive audience and the crowd were watching in anticipation.

He proceeded to show the audience three live toads. Another drum roll and he held a toad in his hand, then lowered it to his mouth. The crowd were putting their hands over their faces. He then swallowed the toad, and showed everyone his empty mouth. I looked on horrified. Another drum roll and he regurgitated the toad, still alive. It was all covered in slime from his gut but the kids loved it. The kids were now laughing more at me, because I was nearly vomiting. How do these people come up with these ideas? Why would you even think about it?

The kids were still laughing, and I decided I had seen enough, because it was anybody's guess what he would get out next. We walked on and made our way through a friendly-looking little village, where we were stopped a few times to buy items. A woman came to me carrying a baby goat, which she let me hold.

On getting back to the hostel we found three Chinese women in the kitchen cooking what smelled and looked like the regurgitated toads. We had bought some fresh baked bread and cheese in the village for a few pence so, we had that in our room instead.

28TH MAY

Our day to fly to Lima, the capital of Peru, so we were up pretty early and had breakfast with the three Chinese women. I think they were having what they couldn't eat last night for breakfast in a bubble and squeak. I don't do bad smells at the best of times, but at six in the morning my barfometer was off the scale. It had been on overdrive, along with my gag reflex, ever since I had left Newcastle Airport.

Our taxi arrived to take us to the airport. To say it didn't look as if it would have a valid MOT would have been an understatement. After four attempts to open the boot, the driver opened it with a screwdriver. We sat in the back and the driver, who could speak no English, gestured for us to keep our feet away from the hole in the floor. As we drove we watched the road whizzing underneath, like Wilma and Fred Flintstone.

When we got to the airport we were stopped on the way in. We stayed in the back while our driver was practically dragged from the car to be checked by security. Once back in we headed for the terminal, and only two attempts and no screwdriver later we were reunited with our luggage.

We found that in Peru you don't need a licence to drive, you just buy the car and off you go. If you want to be a taxi driver you literally paint a sign on the doors of your car, and hey presto you can pick up and charge.

The queue was out the door, and the worrying thing was that the Peruvians were not flying Peruvian airlines. The good thing was, we got straight through. We hoped the floor wouldn't be like the one in the taxi.

Once we had boarded the plane we found it was lovely, and only an hour flight, and we still managed to get breakfast. Well, a piece of Swiss roll and a chicken sandwich.

We landed in Lima, where we were staying at a place called Miraflores. We didn't have a clue where we were going, so because the taxis here were so cheap we jumped in a cab. We had booked our hostel ahead, and when we arrived we found that this area was very middle class. You could tell by the houses and the supermarket. The food was gorgeous and there was a welcome lack of stray dogs, tramps, beggars and women throwing themselves off bridges. The weather wasn't particularly good though, which was a shame because it was only ten minutes' walk from the beach.

29TH MAY

Had a great sleep, but woke up with that feeling of 'it's nearly all over'. Only one country to go. We were checking out today and catching a 1 am flight to Brasilia, the Brazilian capital.

We had breakfast and went into town, to find the town centre packed with hundreds of police. It turned out there was a huge demonstration taking place. There was a woman named Kiako standing for election, and she was being met by huge opposition. Apparently she was the daughter of a previous politician who inflicted cruelty and genocide on his own people. We had recently witnessed the same in Chile.

I know not everyone is of the same opinion when it comes to politics, but at least in England we have a vote and we are not threatened by genocide. There were a lot of very angry people around. Some were holding a quiet and peaceful protest but displaying banners depicting some horrific scenes, while others were very vocal with their demonstrations. I was tempted to throw a stone just so it would kick off, but thought better of it. I was more interested in getting to the posh supermarket for some nice food and something to take on the flight later.

We killed some time sitting in the park with a couple of beers, but after several funny looks we decided we must look like a couple of winos, so we headed back to the hostel. We stayed there until it was time to go to the airport, because we were fed up of sitting in departure lounges. If this is what it's like for Wayne and Colleen, you can keep it.

30TH MAY

We boarded our flight for Brasilia at one in the morning. We didn't have too many flights left now, so we settled down and were looking forward to the last leg of our journey. Just when we were all comfortable and getting ready for take off, the captain told us a fault had been discovered and we all had to get off. We were all ushered like sheep into another queue, and were now worried that we would miss our connecting flight to Rio.

At three in the morning there was another announcement, and we boarded the flight and successfully took off. We had scoffed our sandwiches and were tired and hungry by the time we touched down in Brasilia.

Now that we had missed the connecting flight, we had to think about how we were going to get to Rio. Sod it we thought, we knew we could manage a night on the floor of the airport, and we'd resigned ourselves to this. We collected our luggage and headed to the bar to plan our next move when we heard an announcement 'Can Stephanie and Anthony Hansell please come to Lan desk?' (Lan Airways) so we made our way there. I was wondering if Tony had shoved something in my bag and not told me. I was now paranoid that he was trying to set me up, especially as we had signed our will before we left.

I was relieved that there was nothing in my bag, and even more so to be told that we were being put on the next flight to Rio, which was going to be leaving in a couple of hours - brilliant. The hours whizzed by and we soon boarded the flight. The next time we were on a plane, we would be heading home.

Chapter Thirteen

BRAZIL

We touched down in Rio with a mixture of sadness and excitement, as this was now the last leg of our trip. The airport was manic, but we somehow found where we needed to be for the lift we had arranged. We had been advised to book a lift and not travel through Rio if we didn't know the area. We definitely didn't, so we took the safer option.

Brilliant - our lift from the hostel had not turned up, despite ringing them to inform them of our flights. We looked around the terminal for what looked like a reputable taxi and negotiated a price.

The drive to the hostel was supposed to be less than half an hour and the sights from the window were pretty amazing. We passed some beautiful buildings, though they were covered in graffiti, and some extreme slums. There were people lying on the streets in some areas and heavily-armed police everywhere.

We headed up and up into what looked like mountains. The ride in the car was incredibly uncomfortable, as we had to drive on and off the tram lines to find the best part of the road. If it wasn't tram lines it was cobbled roads, but either way we were thrown all over the place. At one point I was seriously worried that it might be slackening my teeth. I honestly cannot believe how cars manage to drive on these roads without doing serious damage to their suspension. We complain about the size of the speed bumps in Newcastle!

The journey was worth it though, as we arrived at what looked like a nice area. We paid the driver and went inside, to find the hostel was nice enough and the views when we got into the big communal area were magnificent.

From our hostel window we could see Christ the Redeemer (Corcovado) and Sugar Loaf Mountain. There were some monkeys sitting on the windowsill looking in for food, and we were so high up that they were in abundance. From the window we looked down right over one of the favellas (areas of housing in Rio). I wished we had some binoculars, as I would have loved to go into it, but we had been strongly advised not to, and I value my life too much.

As the evening crept in and the light began to fade we sat and watched Christ the Redeemer, which is lit up at night. You could hear a lot of sirens and make out some of the activity going on in the favella, including the odd gunshot. We'll never know if they were warning shots or not. The hostel owners confirmed that they were gunshots and they do have a lot of shootings. They said this one was a pretty safe favella compared to others and that we shouldn't worry too much, just be extra vigilant when we went out. They told us it was OK to walk down into town as long as we were careful with cameras and personal belongings.

We sat at the window teasing the monkeys and got talking to a couple from Canada. The man told us that he would like to visit England, and London in particular, to take in all the sights. He wanted to spend some money and sample some 'good London pubs', but then pointed to his girlfriend and said 'But she doesn't drink'. I said 'That's a shame. If you want to spend some money you could take me, but you would have to go home on the Tuesday'. He just looked at me and didn't get the joke. Canadians just don't do humour.

We retired to bed and had to perform several star jumps again to combat the cold room.

31ST MAY

There was a free breakfast included in the price of the hostel, so we 'doubled up' just in case, telling people 'I'm taking this for the monkeys'. We walked down into town and I have never been happier to be wearing flat sandals. It was practically impossible to walk on the cobbles and just when you thought you had mastered it a tram would come round the corner.

The walk was interesting. We passed some places that appeared to be small blocks of flats but they looked like garages, bizarre. The graffiti was everywhere. Some of it was pretty good though, there were walls with trams painted on them with footballers on board.

We passed a police checkpoint at the entrance of the favela. It was guarded by several police, all pointing their guns to the ground but ready to shoot if they needed to. We made it to the bottom in one piece and caught the Kombi (bus), and then boarded the train from Cosme Velho to travel up the mountain to Christo to see Christ the Redeemer. And you all thought I was past redemption!

The train was very slow as it cut through the forest and we passed many people walking up. It's the most direct route up, I suppose, so a lot of people walk up on the track behind the train. I wished we had done the same, as there were a few too many people on the train for my liking. When it stopped a Brazilian band got on playing instruments, which was just a load of noise to me, then handed round a tray for tips. They practically forced you to put money in. First rip off.

Once at the top it was incredible. It was difficult to get the pictures that you really wanted though, because of the number of people up there. If you lie on the path right under the statue and take one looking up it's a good shot. Loads of people do this and my guess is that one man, probably Chinese, started it off.

Some facts about the statue are:

1. The construction started in 1922.
2. It was finished in 1931.
3. IT weighs over 630 tonnes.
4. It's 130 feet tall.

It's incredible to think that the mountain would take that weight, never mind how they made it.

On the way back we decided to have a beer in the local before we attempted to tackle the walk back up the hill. After two bottles each we were both slurring our words. Either this was seriously strong ale or we had been drugged and were about to be raped and pillaged on the way back. We both felt as if we could take on any 'soft shite' from the favella, as Tony put it. We made it back after an interesting walk through the local neighbourhood. We had come this far and wanted to experience the real Brazil neighbourhood, and it really was OK.

1ST JUNE

The resident dog howled all night and the resident two-year-old decided to throw a temper tantrum at breakfast, so when her mother wasn't watching I gave the tot my 'look' through gritted teeth and clenched my fist at her, which prompted her to stop and go running to her mother. No one had seen me, as they were all watching the mother, who was walking around with her right breast out ready for the screaming tot. Personally I thought she was a bit old to be on the breast, but there again I would rather have a monkey, so what would I know about kids.

We went out to visit the famous steps, which are decorated with tiles. A local artist started tiling them to make the place colourful and interesting - it started with people donating tiles to him. I think at one point he got a 'job lot' of red ones, because a massive area was done in red. Now people from all over the world send him tiles.

CHAPTER THIRTEEN

It's great to try and find a tile from England. Many people send football tiles and we saw loads of them. We didn't find a Newcastle United one. You can sit with this man on the street and watch him paint the tiles and he says he won't give up until it's finished, but the thing is, where would he finish? I think it's a serious case of OCD.

We sat on the balcony at night with a few bottles of beer and watched Christ the Redeemer and listened to the sirens. I also opened the cake from the cupboard that we'd had for breakfast, no one would know it was me so I took the chance.

2ND JUNE

Today would have been my dad's birthday, so Happy Birthday Dad. Had very little sleep again due to the howling dog and screaming child. Came to breakfast and was going to say something, until I saw the one-eyed cleaner hitting the dog with the brush for barking. I was now glad I had eaten her cake. I was hoping the child was going to get it next, but it just kept on screaming. I decided not to say anything, as the thought of the poor dog getting the brush again was too much to cope with.

To catch the local bus, you have to wave it down, pay the driver, go through a turnstile and then hope it stops in the right place. It did stop and we jumped on the train heading to Copacabana Beach. It was pretty busy there even though it was out of season, but the sun was shining, which is apparently all it takes for the bikini-clad volley ball girls to appear. There were men with pink poodles dressed in Speedos (the men, not the poodles), walking up and down the promenade. There were some beautiful big hotels on the beach, all with security guards on the doors. We had a drink on the beach front, where a young lad asked if he could join us. He was hinting that he was a bit skint, but we didn't take the bait and he quickly moved on.

Back walking through the town centre where we caught the train back. Instead of walking up the hill we caught the local bus. The stench of BO was overwhelming and I was glad when we got to our stop.

Back at the hostel we sat out on the balcony watching the vultures, which were bloody enormous. I'd only ever seen vultures in westerns, where they swarm around after the dead. We heard quite a few shots from the favella last night, so there might be a bit of lunch for them. Tony was convinced Rio is not as dangerous as people make out, because, as he pointed out, he was still wearing his five-euro Rolex oyster watch from Benidorm. Personally I can't believe he had taken the risk to wear it. As if some thief is going to rob you and say 'Sorry for the inconvenience, I see it's only a fake from Benidorm, forgive me while I remove this seven inch blade from your wife's throat'.

When Tony took it off his wrist to adjust the time the spring fell off, so he can't wear it now anyway, we are safe. We sat having a glass of wine and watching the vultures with great interest. Ugly things, they would never win any points over the peacock.

3RD JUNE

At breakfast I struggled to decide who to hit first with the brush - the dog, the screaming kid, the cleaner or the new backpacker who had just arrived saying everything was 'awesome' and 'cool'.

'Hello, this place is truly awesome!' she said.

'There's toast and coffee there' I said.

'Awesome, thanks!'

'It's a lovely view from here.'

'Yeah, it's like so cool and awesome!'

'How long you staying?'

'Just tonight, it's a shame because this place is so cool!'

'Good.' (under my breath). It narrows down the people on my brush-hitting list.

I went to our room to get money to go out and found that the watch my mother gave me to go travelling with was in bits. I couldn't think what had happened to it until I came out of the room and immediately saw Tony was wearing his Rolex. He had taken my watch apart to get the part he needed for his. Our lives were at risk again, as he insisted on wearing the fake Rolex. He was ordered to keep his sleeve down and not to even attempt to explain to any robber that it was a fake from Benidorm. He seems to think he would actually be getting one over on the robber, but to me that's as much good as bleeding to death with a smile on your face while your murderer runs off with your fake ten-pound note.

Ten minutes walk from our hostel was the place where Ronnie Biggs had lived, so we went to have a look. It felt strange being outside his front door. I was wondering if Barbara Windsor was there. Tony probably looked like one of Ronnie Knight's mates on account of him the Rolex.

We walked around the Lapa Arches area of town, which was a pretty rough area with loads of undesirable characters lying about on the pavements that didn't move for you to pass. We had to be extra careful, even though there were police everywhere.

The sea wasn't too rough, so we decided to take the ferry to Niterói. It was pretty much the same as this side of Rio, but nice to sample it anyway. The ferry crossing was less than an hour, so it was worth it. There was a nice beach area, which was deserted apart from a few locals doing their washing in the sea. They were sitting near a rock with washing basket, powder, and a scrubbing brush in one hand. It looked like hard work, but what the clothing looked like afterwards I shudder to think. Surely it would be full of salt.

On the way home we saw a huge demonstration involving thousands of firefighters, police, and the military, and from what we could make out they were striking for more money. Same old, same old.

We went to a traditional samba evening in the night, but the drinks were very expensive and it was quite disappointing. To me it was jazz, which is not my favourite, in fact given that I have quite an eclectic collection of music I can say I hate jazz, so we didn't stay long.

We wandered outside, where all the pavement cafés were alive now with music which was free to listen to. There were lots of people dancing in the street, which was what we wanted to see, so we were pleased we had opted to leave when we did.

4TH JUNE

This morning was our last day in the hostel. We were heading home in the evening. We had all day to kill, so we visited the beaches of Ipanema and Copacabana. As expected, the Brazilian beauties were out in force, little thongs and bronzed bare bums, and men in the tiniest of bathing trunks walking their poodles along the front. It's a different world.

We had a coffee and watched the world go by, and were approached by a young lad who was being suspiciously nice. We had been to too many places now and met too many dodgy people to get ripped off on the last day. The lad says to Tony 'You got the time?' to which Tony says 'It's exactly two o'clock by MY Rolex', which meant 'Don't even fucking try and take my Rolex off me on my last day'. It worked, because the lad walked off.

We made our way back to the hostel, and by this time we knew the best route to take. We had everything packed that we were keeping and had dumped most of the stuff we had been wearing for the past seven months. We were both quite subdued at the thought that it was all over.

We were saying goodbye to the hostel staff and guests when more 'cool and awesome' backpackers arrived, so it wasn't a bad time to be leaving. Even the one-eyed cleaner came to say goodbye. We shared a taxi to the airport with another couple. It was quicker going back than it had been coming, another realisation that we had probably been ripped off.

We had been having trouble checking in on line, so we had to do it when we arrived at the airport. I was hoping we could sit together, as it was an eleven-hour flight back to Heathrow. Fortunately we could.

The flight home was long, and although we were excited about seeing everyone again it was sad that the trip was over. When we took off we were in an aisle of four seats with only Tony and me in them, so I had a good sleep across three of them as Tony wasn't bothered.

We landed at Heathrow and got washed and changed and had a couple of pints before flying to Newcastle. Still in backpacker mode, we jumped on the metro to our local club. When we got there all our family and friends were waiting to meet us.

They gave us a wonderful welcome. Thank you to everyone for that.

A BREAKDOWN OF
OUR JOURNEY

1. **Flight to Hong Kong**

2. **Flight to Bangkok** *(Thailand)*

3. **Overnight train to Chang Mai** *(Thailand)*

4. **Local bus to Chang Rai** *(Thailand)*

5. **Flight back to Bangkok** *(Thailand)*

6. **Local bus to Pattaya** *(Thailand)*

7. **Local bus and ferry to Ko Samet Island** *(Thailand)*

8. **Local bus back to Bangkok** *(Thailand)*

9. **Flight to Hanoi** *(Vietnam)*

10. **Overnight bus to Hue** *(Vietnam)*

11. **Local bus to Quehnon** *(Vietnam)*

12. **Local bus to Ho Ann** *(Vietnam)*

13. **Local bus to Nah Trang** *(Vietnam)*

14. **Overnight bus to Saigon** *(Vietnam)*

15. **Local bus to Phnom Penh** *(Cambodia)*

16. **Local bus to Sihanoukville** *(Cambodia)*

17. **Local bus back to Phon Pehn** *(Cambodia)*

18. **Local bus to Sien Reip** *(Cambodia)*

19. **Local bus back to Bangkok** *(Thailand)*

20. **Flight to Penang** *(Malaysia)*

21. Ferry to Langkawi (*Malaysia*)

22. Ferry & Bus to Pa Tong (*Thailand*)

23. Flight to Singapore

24. Flight to Adelaide (*Australia*)

25. Flight to New Zealand (*Christchurch, South Island*)

26. Ferry to North Island, New Zealand

27. Flight to Chile, South America

28. Six day bus journey through the Atacama Desert (*Chile*)

29. Flight to Lima (*capital of Peru*)

30. Flight to Brasilia (*Brazil*)

31. Flight to Rio De Janerio (*Brazil*)

32. Flight to Heathrow (*UK*)

33. Flight to Newcastle (*God's Country*)

Printed in Great Britain
by Amazon